INTERNATIONAL IRON MAN

Billionaire playboy and genius industrialist Tony Stark was kidnapped during a routine weapons test. His captors attempted to force him to build a weapon of mass destruction. Instead, he created a powered suit of armor that saved his life. From that day on, he used the suit to protect the world as the invincible **IRON MAN.**

Recently, Tony discovered that the people who raised him weren't his birth parents...

INTERNATIONAL IRON MAN

ANOTHER STARK INNOVATION

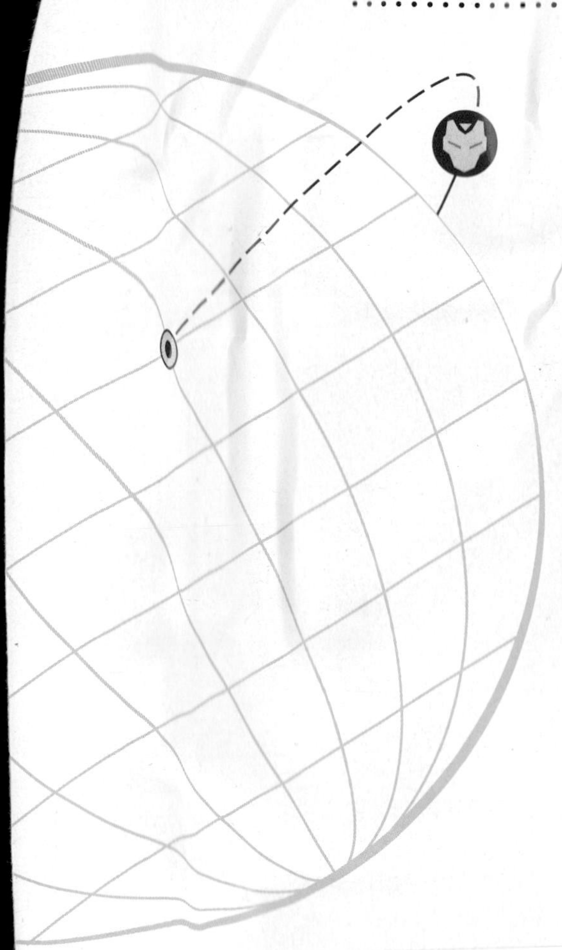

BRIAN MICHAEL BENDIS
WRITER

ALEX MALEEV
ARTIST

PAUL MOUNTS
COLOR ARTIST

VC'S CLAYTON COWLES
LETTERER

ALEX MALEEV
COVER ART

ALANNA SMITH
ASSISTANT EDITOR

TOM BREVOORT
EDITOR

IRON MAN CREATED BY STAN LEE, LARRY LIEBER, DON HECK & JACK KIRBY

COLLECTION EDITOR: **JENNIFER GRÜNWALD**
ASSISTANT EDITOR: **CAITLIN O'CONNELL**
ASSOCIATE MANAGING EDITOR: **KATERI WOODY**
EDITOR, SPECIAL PROJECTS: **MARK D. BEAZLEY**
VP PRODUCTION & SPECIAL PROJECTS: **JEFF YOUNGQUIST**
SVP PRINT, SALES & MARKETING: **DAVID GABRIEL**

EDITOR IN CHIEF: **AXEL ALONSO**
CHIEF CREATIVE OFFICER: **JOE QUESADA**
PRESIDENT: **DAN BUCKLEY**
EXECUTIVE PRODUCER: **ALAN FINE**

INTERNATIONAL IRON MAN. Contains material originally published in magazine form as INTERNATIONAL IRON MAN #1-7. First printing 2017. ISBN# 978-0-7851-9979-3. Published by MARVEL WORLDWIDE, INC., a subsidiary of MARVEL ENTERTAINMENT, LLC. OFFICE OF PUBLICATION: 135 West 50th Street, New York, NY 10020. **Printed in the U.S.A.** DAN BUCKLEY, President, Marvel Entertainment; JOE QUESADA, Chief Creative Officer; TOM BREVOORT, SVP of Publishing; DAVID BOGART, SVP of Business Affairs & Operations, Publishing & Partnership; C.B. CEBULSKI, VP of Brand Management & Development, Asia; DAVID GABRIEL, SVP of Sales & Marketing, Publishing; JEFF YOUNGQUIST, VP of Production & Special Projects; DAN CARR, Executive Director of Publishing Technology; ALEX MORALES, Director of Publishing Operations; SUSAN CRESPI, Production Manager; STAN LEE, Chairman Emeritus. For information regarding advertising in Marvel Comics or on Marvel.com, please contact Vit DeBellis, Integrated Sales Manager, at vdebellis@marvel.com. For Marvel subscription inquiries, please call 888-511-5480. **Manufactured between 6/16/2017 and 7/18/2017 by LSC COMMUNICATIONS INC., KENDALLVILLE, IN, USA.**

10 9 8 7 6 5 4 3 2 1

#1

MONUMENT TO THE SOVIET ARMY.
SOFIA, BULGARIA.
NOW.
HAVE YOU HAD ENOUGH, MISTER STARK?
I THINK HE'S DOWN.
MAYBE HE'S DEAD. I'M NOT READING ANY VITALS.
IT'S IRON MAN, YOU'RE NOT GOING TO READ ANYTHING UNLESS HE WANTS YOU TO.
WHAT'S HE DOING?
MAYBE HE IS DEAD.

MAYBE HE'S PARALYZED.
MAYBE HE'S RETHINKING HIS DISASTROUS LIFE CHOICES THAT LED UP TO THIS HUMBLING MOMENT.

"OR...HE'S DEAD."
TWENTY YEARS AGO.
OH, PLEASE GOD, NO...

UNIVERSITY OF CAMBRIDGE.
PRETTY BUBBLES IN THE AIR!
I'M FOREVER BLOWING BUBBLES!
THEY FLY SO HIGH!
THEY REACH THE SKY!

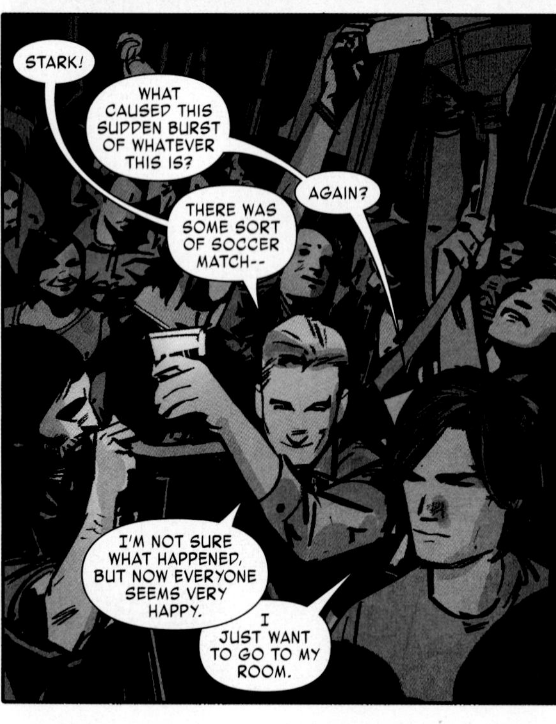
STARK!
WHAT CAUSED THIS SUDDEN BURST OF WHATEVER THIS IS?
AGAIN?
THERE WAS SOME SORT OF SOCCER MATCH--
I'M NOT SURE WHAT HAPPENED, BUT NOW EVERYONE SEEMS VERY HAPPY.
I JUST WANT TO GO TO MY ROOM.

I WISH THEY'D GIVE US A WARNING WHEN THEY DO THIS.
THE SAME "THEY" THAT MAKES US STAY ON CAMPUS INSTEAD OF LIVING IN A NICE--
"THEY"? WHO IS THIS "THEY"? WE'RE THE THEY.
#&$*#, THERE SHE IS.
THERE WHO IS?

I'M FOREVER BLOWING BUBBLES!
PRETTY BUBBLES IN THE AIR!

EXCUSE ME. HOPEFULLY, I WON'T BE RIGHT BACK.
OH, I THINK I HAD A PARTICLE BREAKTHROUGH AND I WAS HOPING YOU'D--
YOU SAY THAT EVERY THREE DAYS.
I THINK I MEAN IT THIS TIME.
THEY REACH THE SKY!
AND LIKE MY DREAMS!

OI! WHO SPILLED ON ME JACKET?!
GET OFF! YOU WANT A GO, MATE?!
BACK OFF, I MEAN IT!
THEY FADE AND DIE!

BLOWING BUBBLES!
OI!
HI.
HI.
I'M TONY.
YEAH? AND?

YOU WANNA GET OUT OF HERE? GET A COFFEE?
NOW?
WELL, YEAH, BEFORE WE GET MURDERED.

THIS IS HARDLY MY KIND OF--OW!
WHACKY

WHACCKK

CRAAACCKKK
AAGH!

I'M GONNA BREAK YOUR FACE!
WHO BROKE YOURS, YOU UGLY TOSSER?!
DID YOU--DID YOU JUST--?
COME ON!

DO YOU KNOW HOW MUCH THIS SUIT--?
UH-OH.
I LOST VISUAL ON THE ANGEL!

WELL.
WELL...
SO, BASICALLY THOSE BODYGUARDS AREN'T TO PROTECT YOU SO MUCH AS TO PROTECT EVERYONE ELSE.

THAT'S MY MOTHER'S IDEA OF GOOD PARENTING.
I KNOW.
I'M TONY.
I'M TRYING TO GET YOU TO SAY YOUR NAME.
YOU *KNOW* MY NAME.
I REALLY DON'T.

YOU'VE BEEN STARING AT ME FOR A WEEK.
YOU DIDN'T ASK ANY OF THE *HUNDREDS* OF PEOPLE AROUND US WHO I AM?
NO.
LIAR.
I DID. WE JUST DON'T KNOW ANY OF THE SAME PEOPLE.

MY NAME IS CASSANDRA GILLESPIE.

DAMMIT!
I *KNEW* YOU HAD A FANTASTIC NAME.
THAT'S A *FANTASTIC* NAME.
AMERICAN.
DON'T HOLD IT AGAINST ME.
I HAD NO IDEA I WAS AMERICAN TILL I WAS BORN.
WHY IS TONY STARK STUDYING HERE IN LONDON?

NOT THE FOOD, I CAN TELL YOU THAT.
IT KEEPS ME FAR AWAY FROM MY PARENTS AND THAT IS A GOOD THING.
I'VE BEEN TO AMERICA.
A FEW TIMES. I DON'T HATE IT.
WHERE'VE YOU BEEN, EXACTLY?
LOS ANGELES. CHICAGO.
YOU REALLY DON'T KNOW WHO I AM?

SHOULD I?
IS YOUR FATHER A BIG DEAL OR SOMETHING?
IS IT--IS HE BONO?
MY MOTHER.
IS *SHE* BONO?

WHAT DOES YOUR MOM DO THAT WARRANTS BODYGUARDS?
I ONLY ASK BECAUSE THEY'RE COMING THIS WAY AND I THINK ONE OF THEM IS ABOUT TO PUNCH ME IN THE FACE SO HARD I PROBABLY WON'T REMEMBER EVER MEETING YOU.

THERE SHE IS!
UGH!
YOU'RE GOING TO GET TASERED.
I'D REALLY RATHER NOT.
I'M NOT JOKING.
NEITHER AM I. CAN YOU REQUEST THAT THEY DON'T?

THEY WON'T LISTEN TO ME! THEY ONLY LISTEN TO MY MOTHER WHO PAYS THEM.
I'VE NEVER BEEN TASERED BEFORE.
YOU'RE NOT GOING TO RUN?
WELL, IF I RUN, *THAT'S* NOT COOL.
AND IF I STAY AND GET TASERED...THAT'S NOT COOL EITHER. I'M IN A BIT OF A PICKLE.
YOU BETTER RUN.

DOES IT HURT?
WHAT?

NO!
AGHHH!
ZZAAATTT

EXCUSE ME!
WHO DO YOU WORK FOR?
LET'S GO!
YOU WORK FOR ME!
I WORK FOR YOUR MOTHER!

WE HAVE HER.
LET GO!
STOP IT!
THE ANGEL IS RETRIEVED.

WORTH IT.
OW.
SCRRRREEEEEEE

THE READING IS REQUIRED!
IT IS THE BARE MINIMUM REQUIREMENT OF THIS CLASS.
SO IF I CALL UPON YOU TO ANSWER A QUESTION, OR TO ENGAGE YOU IN A CONVERSATION ABOUT THE MATERIAL, IT IS BECAUSE I *ASSUME* YOU HAVE DONE THE *BARE MINIMUM...*

...AND ACTUALLY READ THE MATERIAL THAT HAS BEEN ASSIGNED TO YOU.
EXCUSE ME.
PARDON.
NOW, IF YOU *DO NOT* HAVE THE INCLINATION TO DO THE READING, MAYBE THAT SHOULD BE AN INDICATION TO YOUR YOUNG SOUL THAT THIS CLASS IS *NOT* FOR YOU.

SO, LET'S TRY THIS AGAIN. IN CHAPTER THREE, WHAT WAS THE OVERALL THEORY OF UNIFIED FINANCE?
NO ONE?
SERIOUSLY?

SORRY ABOUT THE TASE. I DIDN'T KNOW WHO YOU WERE.
NO WORRIES.
PLEASE DON'T HAVE YOUR DAD KILL ME.
NO PROMISES.

OKAY, NOTHING?
THIS IS *ADVANCED ECONOMICS.* HAS ANYONE READ THE REQUIRED TEXT OR AM I JUST TALKING MYSELF TO

LATER...
ARE YOU UP TO CHAPTER NINE YET?

OH, *UH*, HEY.
I DON'T WANT TO SPOIL IT FOR YOU, BUT... IT'S CRAZY BORING.
NOT TO ME IT'S NOT.
LIAR.
WHY ARE YOU TAKING THE CLASS, THEN? IT'S YOUR MAJOR, NO?
I'M HAVING A MIDLIFE CRISIS, MAYBE.

YOU ARE A RIDDLE, MISTER STARK.
I'M A RIDDLE? YOU'RE THE QUEEN OF RIDDLES.
YOU GOOGLED ME BY NOW.
I DID.
HOW'D THAT GO?

I FOUND OUT YOU'RE A WORLD-CLASS TRAPEZE ARTIST.
IS THERE A TRAPEZE ARTIST WITH MY NAME?
JUST ADMIT YOU TRAPEZE.
THERE'S NOTHING WRONG WITH THAT.
ARE YOU OKAY WITH OUR PARENTS BEING BUSINESS RIVALS?

I DON'T CARE ON ANY LEVEL.
I THINK MY MOTHER MIGHT. WHAT ABOUT YOUR FATHER?
HAVEN'T SPOKEN TO HIM IN, LET'S SEE, WHAT TIME IS IT?
NOON?
OKAY, THAT WOULD MAKE IT FOUR MONTHS.
WHY?

IT SEEMS ONE OF US A SELF-CENTERED, COLDHEARTED SON OF A BITCH WHO ONLY TALKS TO PEOPLE WHO AGREE WITH HIS SPECIFIC WORLD-VIEW AND ISN'T OPEN TO ANY OTHER KIND OF CONVERSATION.

BUT WHAT'S YOUR *FATHER* LIKE?

WELL, THEN, I'M... JEALOUS.
IT'S INTERESTING, NO?
WHAT?
THAT WE, YOU AND I, FIND OURSELVES HERE TOGETHER, AND WE GREW UP IN SUCH SIMILAR AND SPECIFIC ENVIRONMENTS.
SO MUCH OF MY LIFE I HAVE TO JUST KEEP TO MYSELF BECAUSE I THINK NO ONE WOULD UNDERSTAND--
EMPATHIZE.
EXACTLY.

AND I DIDN'T EVEN KNOW ANY OF THIS ABOUT YOU.
CAN I TAKE YOU OUT? PROPERLY?
DO THE TRAINED SEALS HAVE TO COME?

I HAVE AN IDEA BUT IT'S... FORWARD.

OKAY, SICK BURN.
THAT'S IT! WE'RE GETTING MARRIED.
WE NEED TO TALK ABOUT THIS OR THIS ISN'T HAPPENING.
OR *WHAT* ISN'T HAPPENING?
THIS. US. EVEN LUNCH.

I'M NOT MY FATHER. ON ANY LEVEL.
HONESTLY, WE'RE NOT EVEN SPEAKING.
I PAY MY OWN WAY.

I'M VERY CLOSE WITH MY FAMILY.

I ASKED YOU TO MARRY ME, LIKE, FIVE MINUTES AGO.
HOW FORWARD CAN IT BE?

HAVE DINNER WITH MY FAMILY.

I UNDERSTAND.
IT'S--IT'S FORWARD.
WE HARDLY KNOW EACH OTHER.
BUT I THOUGHT--

BUT YOU THOUGHT IT FELT LIKE WE DID KNOW EACH OTHER.

YES.
THAT--*THAT* IS WHAT I WAS THINKING.

OKAY, SURE.

"*SURE*" MEANS...?

LET'S GO TO DINNER!
THE ENTIRE FAMILY. WHAT'S THE WORST THAT COULD HAPPEN?
I SAY SOMETHING STUPID, YOUR MOTHER HAS ME KILLED AND FIVE OR SIX MONTHS LATER MY FATHER FINALLY FIGURES OUT I AM NO LONGER ON THE PLANET.

DID YOU CALL UNCLE FABRICE?
NO, MAMA.
HE LIVES FIFTEEN MINUTES FROM YOUR CAMPUS.
I'LL TRY. WE'RE VERY BUSY. THE SCHOOLWORK IS OVERWHELMING.
BUT YOU'RE NOT TOO BUSY TO MEET A NICE YOUNG MAN.

WE'RE IN CLASSES TOGETHER.
A MAN SHOULD PAY HIS OWN WAY, NO?
SIR?
HE IS.
GIORGIO, BE NICE.

AND WHAT DO *YOU* DO, MISTER GILLESPIE?
WILL YOU BE JOINING US FOR DINNER, ALEXANDER?
I'M HERE. I'M CATCHING EVERY RIVETING, PASSIVE-AGGRESSIVE WORD.

WHAT ARE YOUR PLANS, TONY?
WELL, I'M KEEPING MY HEART AND MIND OPEN.
THE WORLD IS CHANGING SO QUICKLY THAT BY THE TIME WE GRADUATE--
SO YOU **HAVE** NO PLANS?
PAPA!

SIR, I ALREADY HAVE A HANDFUL OF PATENTS UNDER MY NAME.
I USE THAT MONEY TO, AS YOU SAY, *"PAY MY OWN WAY."*
I'M JUST TRYING TO EXPRESS TO YOU THAT I AM AWARE OF HOW QUICKLY THE GEOPOLITICAL LANDSCAPE IS CHANGING AND HOW MUCH I KNOW THESE CHANGES MEAN TO THE PROSPECTS FOR FUNDING AND--

ALEXANDER, PUT THE PHONE AWAY NOW!
I FEEL LIKE WE'RE BONDING.

DO YOU WANT TO SEE THE CAMPUS?
I THINK YOUR FATHER IS TIRED.

TONY, YOU'RE TO COME TO VISIT US AT OUR HOME.
I APPRECIATE THAT, MA'AM.
BUT I DON'T THINK YOUR HUSBAND IS ALL THAT INTERESTED IN--
DON'T BE SILLY. COME STAY WITH US.
I PROMISE YOU IT'LL BE FAR MORE RELAXING THAN YOUR LITTLE ROOM AT SCHOOL.

SCREEEEEEVRROOOOMMM

SCREEEEEEE

HAIL HYDRA!
BUDDABUDDABUDDABUDDA

AGH!
OH GOD!
BUDDABUDDABUDDABUDDABUDDABUDDABUDDABUDDA
BUDDABUDDABUDDABUDDABUDDABUDDABUDDABUDDA
GUAAAGH!
AAGGH!
BUDDABUDDABUDDABUDDABUDDABUDDABUDDABUDDA

STAY DOWNAAGH!
BUDDABUDDABUDDABUDDABUDDABUDDABUDDABUDDA

BAM BAM BAM

CRRAASHH

TONY!

YOU BETRAYED OUR CAUSE, GILLESPIE.
YOU WERE WARNED THIS WOULD HAPPEN.
YOU SOLD WEAPONS TO OUR OPPRESSORS, AND NOW YOU AND YOUR FAMILY DIE.

BAM

BAM

BAM

BAM

HAIL HYDRA!

BAM
AGH!

TONY!

AAAAAAAGGH!
HAIL--

SPACKKK

POLICE
MISTER STARK?
ARE YOU IN THERE?
OF COURSE HE'S IN THERE.
HE LIVES IN THERE.
REMOVE THE FACE PLATE.
HE'S NOT GOING TO LIKE IT.

HE'S ALIVE.
I'M NOT GOING TO DO THIS.
I'M NOT GOING TO FIGHT YOU...
...CASSANDRA.
GOOD.
I DON'T WANT TO FIGHT YOU EITHER, TONY.
BUT HELL IF I'M GOING TO LET YOU STAND BETWEEN ME AND WHAT I HAVE COMING.
AND HELL IF I'M GOING TO DO IT AGAIN.
AND TONY, MY DARLING, FIGHTING *ME* ISN'T GOING TO GET YOU ANY CLOSER TO FINDING OUT WHO YOUR REAL FATHER IS.
THAT I CAN PROMISE YOU.

#2

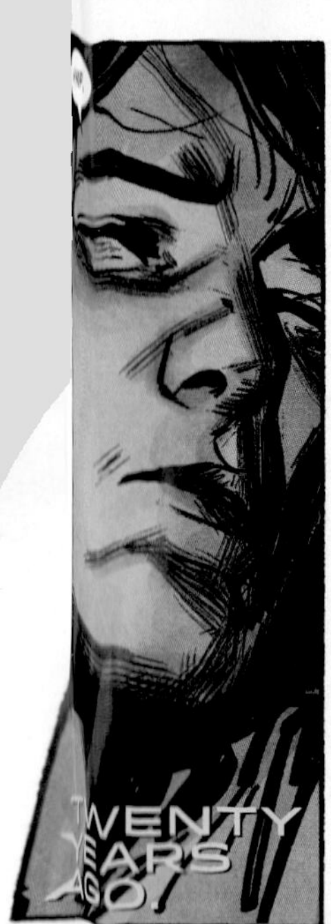
TWENTY YEARS AGO.

OW.

NOT LONDON.

NO LABEL.

UM...
MRS. GILLESPIE?

SORRY.

THAT WAS VERY BRAVE OF YOU TONIGHT, ANTHONY.
WHAT-- WHAT WAS ALL THAT?
IT IS, AND ALWAYS WILL BE, A VERY DANGEROUS WORLD.

WHAT--WHAT DOES THAT MEAN, EXACTLY?
NO, THANK YOU.
DRINK?

IT'LL HELP THE ARM.
EVEN WITH THE PAIN KILLERS?
ESPECIALLY WITH THE PAIN KILLERS.

OOF.
WOW.

MY QUESTION TO YOU IS: WHY ARE YOU SO BRAVE, TO DO WHAT YOU DID?

UM, WHO, MM, BANDAGED ME?
HOW DID I GET HERE? HOW LONG HAVE I BEEN--?
HAVE ANOTHER. ANSWER MY QUESTION.

I DIDN'T EVEN REALIZE WHAT I WAS DOING UNTIL IT WAS OVER.

BAM BAM BAM

INSTINCTS.
I GUESS.
I WAS AN ORPHAN.
I GREW UP IN AN ORPHANAGE.
IN RETROSPECT, IT WAS A PRISON, REALLY.
THE STREETS OF SOFIA, BULGARIA, NO LESS.
I KNEW I HAD TO EARN MY PLACE IN THE WORLD.
AND I DID.
I SPENT MOST OF MY LIFE FIGHTING.
FIGHTING FOR FOOD, FIGHTING FOR A MOMENT JUST TO HAVE A THOUGHT, FIGHTING JUST TO GET TO THE NEXT DAY...
IT WAS TOO MUCH. I'D RATHER SLEEP IN THE STREET. MAKE MY OWN WAY.
I KNOW THAT IS WHERE I LEARNED TO FIGHT.
BUT YOU. SON OF HOWARD STARK. WHERE DID YOU LEARN THIS?
YOU REALLY SLEPT ON THE STREET?

GIORGIO COMES FROM A VERY LARGE FAMILY. VERY CRAZY.
BUT WHEN MY GIORGIO TOLD HIS FATHER HE WAS IN LOVE WITH ME, THAT MAN, CRAZY AS HE WAS, HE BROUGHT ME IN...INTO THEIR WORLD.
AND SUDDENLY, FOR THE FIRST TIME IN MY ENTIRE LIFE, I HAD A FAMILY.

I HAD HOPED, ONE DAY, I COULD DO THE SAME FOR WHATEVER YOUNG MAN CASSANDRA BROUGHT HOME.
BUT THEN, AS SHE GREW AND GREW, I THOUGHT: WHAT MAN COULD EVER BE ENOUGH?
WHAT MAN DESERVES HER?
AND THESE IDIOTS SHE BROUGHT HOME FROM SCHOOL.
YOU SHOULD HAVE SEEN THEM.

AND THEN COMES YOU.
AN AMERICAN, OF ALL THINGS.
A STARK. THE COMPETITION.

YOU SAVED MY LIFE.
AND YOU SAVED THE LIFE OF MY ENTIRE FAMILY.
REGARDLESS OF ALL THE OTHER PIECES OF YOU...
...THAT HAS TO BE GOOD ENOUGH, RIGHT?

I AM FOREVER AND ALWAYS IN YOUR DEBT.

ARE YOU OKAY, CASSANDRA?
SO BRAVE.
YES, MAMA.

HEY.

HELL OF A FIRST DATE.
ONE FOR THE RECORD BOOKS.

I CAN'T TOP THIS... JUST SO YOU KNOW.
WELL, NOT WITH THAT ATTITUDE.
OW.
SORRY.

UH, WHERE ARE WE EXACTLY?
SPAIN. MY FAMILY HOME.
SPAIN?
WE TOOK A PRIVATE PLANE TO A FAMIL DOCTOR AND THEN HERE.

PLEASE.
IT'S *NEVER* HAPPENED BEFORE.
NOT TO US.
I'M NOT CAVALIER. I'M JUST HAPPY WE'RE ALL OKAY.
THANK GOD YOU WERE THERE.

I--
I AM FREAKED OUT.

WE HAVE SCHOOL TOMORROW.

I DON'T THINK I LIKE HOW CAVALIER YOU'RE BEING WITH WHAT HAPPENED.
WE'LL BE BACK IN TIME.
BY THE WAY, NICELY DONE WITH MY MOTHER.

NO ONE IS BEING CAVALIER.
I THINK I KILLED A GUY.
IF YOU DID, HE WAS A BAD, BAD GUY.
HOW OFTEN DOES THAT HAPPEN?

UNIVERSITY OF CAMBRIDGE.
TWO DAYS LATER.

@#$@.

A HYDRA ATTACK ON A KNOWN TERRORIST'S WEAPONS DEALER? IT'S NEWS.
SECURITY CAMERAS CAUGHT THE WHOLE THING. IT WAS ON CNN.
WELL, I-- I DIDN'T KNOW THAT.

YES.
BECAUSE YOU'VE BEEN TOO BUSY GALLIVANTING ALL OVER EUROPE WITH THOSE PIECES OF EURO-$@$@$.
DON'T DO THIS.
GET IN!
NO.
TAKE HIM.

SCREEE

LET'S GO, TONY.
DAD?
RIGHT NOW.
WHERE ARE WE GOING?

HOME.
I AM HOME. I LIVE HERE.
DON'T BE A SMART-ASS.
WHAT ARE YOU DOING HERE?
I KNOW YOU'RE SMART ENOUGH TO FIGURE THAT OUT ON YOUR OWN.

HOW DO YOU KNOW WHAT HAPPENED TO ME?
ARE YOU HAVING ME FOLLOWED AGAIN?
YES. BUT IT WAS ON THE NEWS ANYWAY.
IT WAS?

STOP IT.
STOP-- OW!

OW!
@#$@#$!

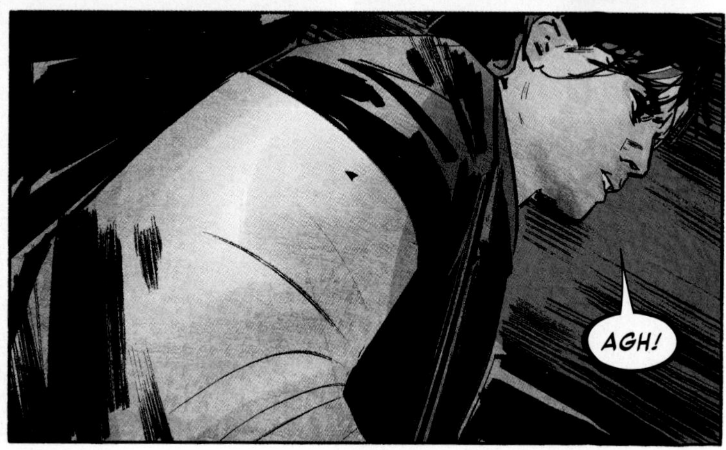
AGH!

TAKE THIS.
IT'LL HELP.
WE'LL HAVE A REAL DOCTOR LOOK AT YOUR ARM BACK IN THE STATES.

NOT SOME EURO MOB DOCTOR HANDING OUT PILLS AND LEECHES.
YOU DON'T KNOW WHAT YOU'RE TALKING ABOUT.

DO YOU KNOW WHAT A HONEY POT IS?
IT'S A SPY-TRADE TERM.
GORGEOUS GIRL SUCKS IN A GUY.
GETS HIM TO DO EXACTLY WHAT SHE WANTS EXACTLY WHEN SHE WANTS HIM TO DO IT.

OH MY GOD!
I PURSUED *HER.*

DID YOU?

SOFIA, BULGARIA. TODAY.
OKAY, SO, LET'S TRY THIS AGAIN...
CASSANDRA GILLESPIE, NO MORE FIGHTING...
YOU'RE UNDER ARREST.

IF I COULD ARREST YOU FOR MESSING ME UP FOR ALL WOMEN, I'D DO IT...
...BUT I'LL SETTLE FOR ILLEGAL TRADE OF ILLEGAL WEAPONS TO KNOWN INTERNATIONAL TERRORISTS.
INTERESTING.
SADLY, I DON'T ACKNOWLEDGE YOUR AUTHORITY OVER ME.

WELL, I DON'T MEAN TO TELL YOU YOUR BUSINESS, BUT YOU SHOULD.
I'M KIND OF A BIG DEAL.
HERE'S WHAT IS GOING TO HAPPEN NOW...

I'M GOING TO TAKE YOUR ARMOR AS COMPENSATION FOR YOU INTERRUPTING MY BUSINESS THIS EVENING.
I'M GOING TO LET YOU LIVE, BECAUSE IF I KILL YOU, ALL OF YOUR LITTLE SUPER HERO FRIENDS WILL COME LOOKING FOR ME AND THAT IS JUST BAD FOR BUSINESS.
BUT I AM TELLING YOU, TONY.

PEOPLE.
YOU HAVE PEOPLE YOU CARE ABOUT.

I'LL START REMOVING THEM FROM EXISTENCE.
AND I'LL EVEN MAKE IT LOOK LIKE YOU DID IT.
BUT IF YOU LEAVE ME AND MINE ALONE, FOR OLD TIMES' SAKE, I'LL LEAVE YOU ALONE.

CASSANDRA, I'M NOT GOING TO LET YOU SELL WEAPONS TO TERRORISTS.
IT'S NOT GOING TO HAPPEN. YOU *KNOW* THAT.

TONY.
CASSANDRA.
YOU HID FROM ME FOR TWENTY YEARS.
I'M VERY GOOD AT IT.
ALSO, YOU WEREN'T LOOKING.
BUT I GO LOOKING FOR MY BIOLOGICAL FATHER AND I FIND YOU.

I KNOW.
ARE YOU MY FATHER?
I KNOW YOU WON'T BELIEVE ME, BUT YOU'RE BETTER OFF NO KNOWING WHO YOUR FATHER IS.

I PROMISE YOU...
...IF YOU COME LOOKING FOR ME, IF I CATCH EVEN A GOOGLE SEARCH COMING FROM YOUR PART OF THE WORLD, I WILL START TAKING THINGS FROM YOU.

"TERRORISTS." YOU WITH THE LABELS.
MANY PEOPLE CONSIDER YOU MORE OF A TERRORIST THAN THE PEOPLE I SELL TO.
WELL, TO BE FAIR, MOST PEOPLE ARE FAIRLY STUPID.
AND I FIND THERE IS AN ANTI-FACIAL-HAIR BIAS OUT THERE.
PEOPLE DON'T TALK ABOUT IT ENOUGH, BUT IT'S... REAL.

I ACTUALLY DO BELIEVE YOU.
BUT HOW ABOUT A HINT?

WALK AWAY, TONY.
IS IT VICTOR VON DOOM?
TAKE THE ARMOR. LEAVE THE MAN.

CASSANDRA, HOW DO YOU THINK THIS WILL END FOR YOU?
YOU'RE SO SMART!
YOU **KNOW** HOW THIS ENDS!

CASSANDRA!

CASSANDRA...

CLANGG
FRIDAY?
GO!
ALL SYSTEMS READY, BUT--

POWER CELLS LOW.
FSSHAAAMM

WE HAVE YOU SURROUNDED, STARK!
YOU KNOW I'M, LIKE, THE LEADING ARMOR WEAPONS SYSTEM EXPERT ON THE PLANET, RIGHT?
YEAH, SO?
SERIOUSLY, AREN'T YOU EVEN A LITTLE JAZZED TO MEET ME? YOU OWE YOUR WHOLE DEAL TO ME.
GO TO HELL.
NOT NICE.

FFSSSHHTTZZAATTT

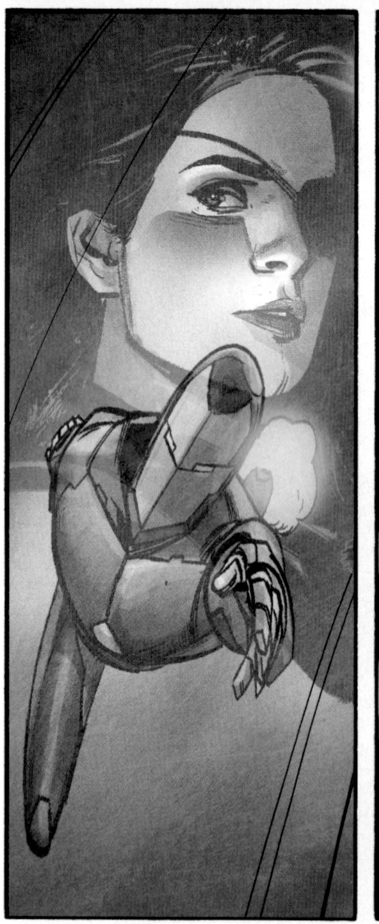

GUY'S GOOD.
ZZAAZZZ
ZZAAZZZ
IT'S IRON MAN! HE WASN'T LYING, HE INVENTED THIS.

FRIDAY!
PUT EVERYTHING IN THE SHIELDS. I'M GOING AFTER HER.
YOU WON'T GET FAR UNDER THIS LEVEL OF ATTACK.
SURE, I WILL.
I HAVE YOU.

AGH!
I TOLD YOU.

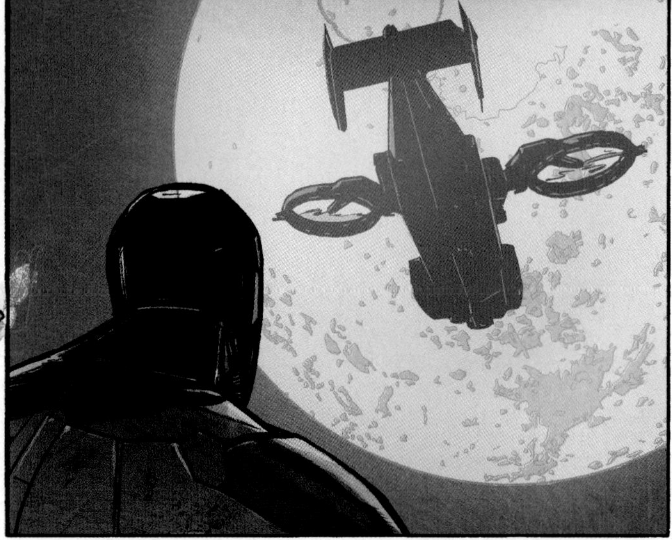

POWER CELLS ALMOST DEPLETED. HULL DAMAGE IS SEVERE.

DON'T DAMAGE THE ARMOR TOO MUCH.
SHE WANTS IT.
FFSSSHHTTZZAATT
FRIDAY?

POWER CELLS AT ONE PERCENT.

FRABOOOM

CASSANDRA!

FRIDAY, WHERE DID SHE GO?
WHERE'S THE COPTER?

IF WE HAVE CLOAKING TECH, WE HAVE TO ASSUME SHE DOES, TOO.
I INVENTED CLOAK TECH!
FIND HER.
SHE'S GONE.

AND YOU'RE STILL SURROUNDED BY MANDROIDS OF A MUCH HIGHER CALIBER THAN WE WERE PREPARED FOR.
HULL BREACH IMMINENT.

POWER CELLS DEPLETED. YOU CANNOT FLY. YOU CAN'T WIN THIS FIGHT AND YOU CAN'T RETREAT.
THE HULL HAS BEEN BREACHED.

#3

THE HULL HAS BEEN BREACHED.
I HEARD YOU, FRIDAY!
EVASIVE ACTION REQUIRED.
SOFIA, BULGARIA. TODAY.
HOLD ON.
HOLD ON?
YOU ARE STILL SURROUNDED BY MANDROIDS OF A MUCH HIGHER CALIBER THAN WE WERE PREPARED FOR.
POP THE FACE-PLATE.
I'M SORRY?
FOLD THE ARMOR.
WE'RE SURRENDERING.
THEY ARE GOING TO KILL YOU.

MAYBE.
MAYBE NOT.
THEY WANT YOUR ARMOR AND THEY CLEARLY DON'T CARE WHAT HAPPENS TO YOU IN THE PROCESS OF GETTING IT.
I KNOW, FRIDAY.
I'VE BEEN HERE THE ENTIRE TIME.
THEY ARE TERRORIST ASSASSIN MANDROIDS--
YOU'RE MY PROGRAM, FRIDAY.
DO WHAT I SAY!
MY PRIMARY FUNCTION, AS YOU WELL KNOW, IS TO KEEP YOU ALIVE AND IN AS FEW PIECES AS POSSIBLE.
FRIDAY! I HAVE A PLAN.
YOU HAVE A HUNCH.
CAN WE WIN THIS MANDROID FIGHT AS IS?
OH, HELL NO.
THEN POP THE ARMOR!
I'M CALLING THE AVENGERS.
POP THE @#$@#$%# ARMOR!
POP
HI.
TONY STARK.
AND YOU ARE?

STARK MANSION.
TWENTY YEARS AGO.

IS HE STILL SLEEPING?
HE'S OUTSIDE, MR. STARK.

REALLY? DID HE SLEEP?
I JUST GOT HERE.

HOW'S THE ARM?
IT HURTS.
YOU'RE LUCKY YOU'RE ALIVE, TONY.
YOU'RE WRONG ABOUT CASSANDRA, DAD.
OKAY.
EXCEPT I'M NOT.

THE GILLESPIES ARE RUTHLESS BASTARDS.
INTERNATIONAL WEAPONS DEALERS.
SO ARE YOU.
WELL, *THAT'S* NOT NICE.
THEY SAID *YOU* WERE THEIR COMPETITION.
THEY SELL TO THE PEOPLE I WOULD *NEVER* SELL TO.

OH! *WELL*, THEN...
THEY YELLED OUT *"HAIL HYDRA."*
LET'S REWIND. IT WAS HYDRA THAT ATTACKED YOU?
YOU KILLED ONE OF THEM? YOU ACTUALLY DID THAT?

I THINK SO.
WHAT ARE YOU INSINUATING?
AND THEY HAPPENED TO ATTACK YOU THE ONE NIGHT YOU WENT OUT ON THE TOWN WITH THE GILLESPIES.
YOU'RE SAYING IT *WASN'T* HYDRA.
I'M SAYING: INTERESTING TIMING.
COME ON.

BOY MEETS GIRL. GIRL INTRODUCES BOY TO FAMILY.
BOTH HAPPEN TO BE THE OFFSPRING OF RUTHLESS COMPETITORS IN A VERY RUTHLESS GAME.
BUT OH, NO! TERRORISTS ATTACK.
BOY, WHO NEVER DID ANYTHING LIKE THIS BEFORE IN HIS LIFE...SAVES THE DAY?

YOU WEREN'T THERE, DAD.
HAVE I DESCRIBED ANY OF IT INCORRECTLY?
YOU WEREN'T THERE.
I KNOW YOU CAN'T STAND ME RIGHT NOW...BUT IT DOESN'T MEAN I'M WRONG.
YOU FELL FOR A HONEY POT.

YOU WON'T DO IT AGAIN.
AND I WON'T TELL MOM.

NOW.
TAKE IT.
IT'S YOURS.
IT'S A TRICK.
KILL HIM.

MS. GILLESPIE SAID NOT TO.
BUT SHE DIDN'T THINK HE'D FOLD.
NOT FOLDING.
YOU HAD ME FAIR AND SQUARE.
SHUT UP.
SHUTTING UP.

HOW DO WE KNOW THIS ARMOR OF YOURS ISN'T RIGGED TO BLOW?
BECAUSE I'M STANDING RIGHT HERE AND I'D NEVER KILL ME.
I'M A REALLY HUGE FAN OF MINE.

I SAID: SHUT UP!
KTANG

@#$!
TAKE THE ARMOR.
I'LL STAY HERE WITH HIM, AND IF HE TRIES ANYTHING OR IF ANYTHING GOES FISHY WITH THE ARMOR, I'LL WHACK HIM.
I FEEL LIKE I'M GETTING THE CRAP END OF THIS DEAL.
I'LL CATCH UP. GO.

THE LOCAL POLICE ARE GOING TO FIND US ANY SECOND.
I'D WORRY MORE ABOUT THE AVENGERS, BUT SURE, I'M SURE THE BULGARIAN POLICE ARE QUITE SOMETHING, TOO.

HEY, YOU LIKE YOUR SPINE WHERE IT IS?
WELL, AGH, I'VE NEVER GIVEN IT A LOT OF THOUGHT.
WELL, I'D START TAKING THIS A LITTLE MORE SERIOUSLY.
AGH! YOU KNOW, SUDDENLY I DO.

FOR WHAT IT'S WORTH... SORRY.
I REALLY AM A BIG FAN, MISTER STARK.
BUT YOU DON'T KNOW WHEN TO SHUT UP.
THEY SAY IT'S PART OF MY CHARM.
IT AIN'T.
HOW MUCH IS SHE PAYING YOU GUYS?

STOP TALKING.
JUST WANT TO KNOW WHAT THE GOING RATE IS.
I MEAN... FLYING A SUIT LIKE THAT IS NOT RUN-OF-THE-MILL THUG WORK.
YOU A PILOT?

WHY DID YOU GIVE UP YOUR ARMOR?
I'VE GOT OTHERS.

WORD IS SHE'S NEVER LEFT SOMEONE WHO MESSED WITH HER ALIVE BEFORE.
YOU TWO REALLY HAVE A HISTORY, HUH?
OH, YEAH.

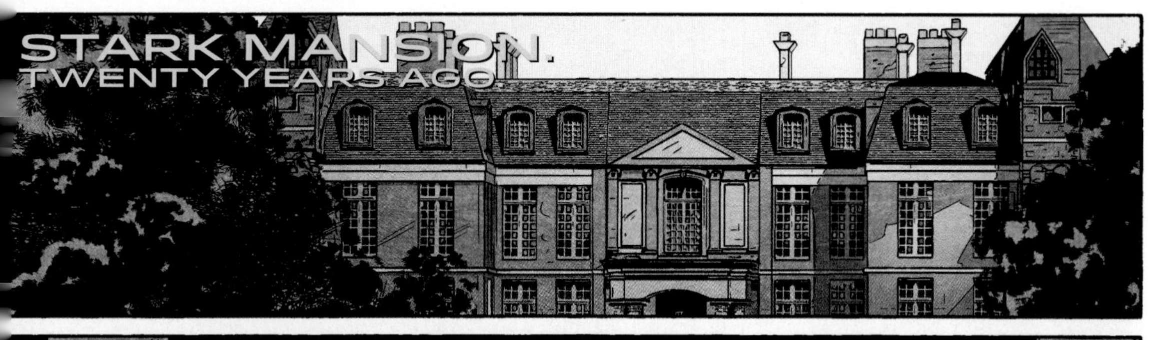
STARK MANSION.
TWENTY YEARS AGO.

WHERE IS HE?
NOT HERE.

WHAT?!
WHEN WERE YOU GOING TO TELL ME?
WE JUST FIGURED IT OUT, SIR.
WE WERE JUST DECIDING TO WAKE YOU.

WELL...
WE KNOW *WHERE* HE'S GOING.

UNIVERSITY OF CAMBRIDGE.

PLEASE STAY BACK WHILE WE SWEEP THE APARTMENT, MS. GILLESPIE.
I KNOW THE DRILL.

CLEAR.
CLEAR.
MAY I RELIEVE MYSELF NOW?

YES, MA'AM.
DO YOU NEED US TO GET YOU ANY--?
SLAM

IT'S OKAY TO CRY.

TONY?!
HOW-- HOW DID YOU JUST--
I DO IT ALL THE TIME.
WHISPER.
FOR BOTH OF US.

CLOAKING DEVICE.
I MADE IT.
YOU *MADE* IT?
I TOLD YOU I HAD PATENTS.

A CLOAKING DEVICE?
IT ONLY WORKS FOR A MINUTE AND I THINK IT CAUSES CANCER... BUT I'M WORKING ON IT.
WHERE THE HELL HAVE YOU *BEEN?*
TRAPPED IN AMERICA WITH MY FATHER.
HE SAW WHAT HAPPENED ON TV AND PUT ME IN HIS VERSION OF JAIL.
I WAS STUCK IN OUR NEW YORK MANSION ALL DAY EVERY DAY WITH NOTHING BUT EVERY VIDEO GAME KNOWN TO MAN AND EVERYTHING THE INTERNET HAD TO OFFER.
SOUNDS BARBARIC.
I'M SORRY.
I GOT BACK HERE AS SOON AS I COULD.
YOU'VE BEEN GONE FOR WEEKS.
IT TOOK ME--I HAD TO STAY OFF THE GRID TO STAY AWAY FROM MY DAD.
DO YOU KNOW WHAT S.H.I.E.L.D. IS?

I'VE HEARD OF IT.
WELL, IT'S A WORLD PEACEKEEPING TASK FORCE/SPY AGENCY AND MY DAD KIND OF INVENTED IT.
I HAD TO GET ALL THE WAY FROM AMERICA TO HERE WITHOUT ANYONE NOTICING.
OLD SCHOOL.
LIKE... *MAYFLOWER* OLD SCHOOL.
I'M SHAKING.
HOW-- HOW DID YOU GET HERE?
I'M TELLING YOU...I STOWED AWAY.
I WORKED MY WAY BACK HERE.
REALLY?
AND THEN I HAD TO COVERTLY FOLLOW YOU AROUND TO FIGURE OUT YOUR SCHEDULE AND THEN BREAK INTO YOUR APARTMENT WHEN I KNEW YOU WEREN'T HOME AND THEN FIGURE OUT A WAY TO HIDE FROM YOUR BODYGUARDS.
AND, WOW, DOES THAT SOUND SUPER STALKY WHEN YOU SAY IT OUT LOUD.
MISS GILLESPIE?

CAN I HAVE A @#$@#$@# MOMENT TO MY #$%#$% SELF, PLEASE?!

SO WHAT DO WE DO NOW?

WE RUN AWAY TOGETHER.

I CAN'T LEAVE MY FAMILY.
I KNOW.
AND I'M JEALOUS.
AND I HAVE NO RIGHT TO SAY THIS...BUT I'M PRETTY SURE YOU KNOW YOU'RE LIVING IN A PRISON.

THIS-- THIS IS ALL A PRISON.
COME WITH ME.

NO.
BUT--
YOU BROUGHT HIS ARMOR HERE? TO MY COMPOUND?
YOU TOLD US TO BRING YOU HIS ARMOR.
NOT *HERE!*

THIS IS THE BEST PERSONAL WEAPONS SYSTEM IN THE WORLD.
HE GAVE IT TO YOU SO HE COULD TRACK YOU WITH IT.
IS IT BROADCASTING *ANYTHING?*
THERE'S NO SIGNAL EMANATING FROM IT.

NO.
MA'AM, WE'RE NOT STUPID.
IF IT WAS EMANATING ANY KIND OF ENERGY SOURCE OR FREQUENCY, WE WOULD HAVE DESTROYED IT.

NO.
GET IT OUT OF HERE.
TAKE IT TO THE WAREHOUSE UP NORTH.
I'M SORRY?
YES, MA'AM.

HE JUST... GAVE IT TO YOU?
WELL, WE WERE PRETTY MUCH ABOUT TO TAKE IT OFF OF HIM.
WE HAD HIM, MA'AM.

UH-HUH.

THIS IS HOW IT HAPPENS.

THIS IS A NICE BATHROOM.

I'VE ALWAYS HAD MONEY, BUT I NEVER SAW THE NEED TO MAKE A BATHROOM LIKE THIS.
IT'S LIKE MAKING A SHRINE TO YOUR POOPING.
DAMN YOU.
YOU DON'T NEED TO DO THAT.
SO THE ARMOR WAS TRACKING.
HOW? THERE WAS NO SIGNAL, NO--
OF COURSE.
I'M SMARTER THAN EVERYBODY.
THIS COMPOUND IS MY FAVORITE PLACE ON EARTH.
SURE. IT'S GORGEOUS.
NOW I HAVE TO KILL YOU TO KEEP IT.
I HAVE TO.
TAP
NOT REALLY.
WAIT.

TAP
TAP
CAMOUFLAGE.
YOUR ARMOR HAS CAMOUFLAGE THAT EXTENSIVE?
PUT THE GUN AWAY AND WE'LL TALK.
PUT THE GUN AWAY?
YOU'RE WEARING A *TANK.*
YOU KNOW I COULD TAKE THAT RIGHT OUT OF YOUR HAND AND TAKE YOU RIGHT TO S.H.I.E.L.D.
RIGHT NOW.
SO... PUT THE GUN DOWN.
AND SIT.
HERE?
WE'RE GOING TO DO THIS *HERE?*
RIGHT.
HERE.

AUCKLAND, NEW ZEALAND.
TWENTY YEARS AGO.
WHAT ARE YOU THINKING, CAPTAIN STARK?
NO.
NO?
YOU GET ONE "WHAT ARE YOU THINKING" A DAY.
YOU USED YOURS UP AT LUNCH.
YOU HAVEN'T SPOKEN SINCE LUNCH.
MY MOTHER TOLD ME THE KEY TO A HAPPY RELATIONSHIP IS NOT HAVING TO TALK.
TO BE ABLE TO SIT IN QUIET.
CUT THE @#$@#, CAPTAIN.

I WAS THINKING I COULD MAKE THIS BOAT FLY.
THEN IT WOULDN'T BE A BOAT, IT WOULD BE A PLANE.
I THINK I COULD CREATE A PROPULSION SYSTEM THAT COULD MAKE IT GO FROM UNDERWATER TO ON WATER TO IN THE SKY WITHOUT CHANGING GEARS.
I HAVE IT PRETTY MUCH LAID OUT IN MY HEAD.

DO YOU NEED TO GO WRITE IT DOWN?
YOU'RE NOT AFRAID YOU'LL FORGET IT?
NO, I HAVE IT.
WHY WOULD I FORGET IT?

OKAY, GENIUS CAPTAIN...HOW ABOUT WE SLEEP IN A HOTEL TONIGHT?
OOOH. ALL RIGHT.
AND I'LL TELL YOU WHAT I WAS REALLY THINKING.
I WAS THINKING HOW MY DAD THOUGHT THAT YOU WERE A *"HONEY POT."*
THAT'S NICE.

NO. IT MEANS HE THOUGHT YOU WERE--THAT YOU WERE TRYING TO SEDUCE ME.
I WAS.
FOR YOUR PARENTS.
USING ***ME*** TO GET TO ***HIM.***

MY DAD.
MR. WRONG.

WHAT?

ONLY IN THE BEGINNING.

ONLY IN THE BEGINNING OF WHAT?

I WAS TO MEET YOU AND BRING YOU INTO MY FAMILY AND GET YOU TO TALK ABOUT YOUR FATHER.
BUT THAT WAS B-BEFORE--
BEFORE WHAT?

BEFORE I FELL FOR YOU.
FOR REAL.

TELL ME.
WHAT?
WHAT DO YOU WANT FROM ME, TONY?
YOU WANT ME TO SAY I'M SORRY FOR SOMETHING A STUPID CHILD DID A MILLION YEARS AGO?
COME ON, CASSANDRA.
WE'RE ALL GROWN UP NOW. WE CAN TALK LIKE ADULTS.
WHO IS HE? WHERE IS HE?

I FIND OUT THE MAN WHO HAS BEEN RAISING ME/ TORTURING ME FOR MY ENTIRE LIFE WAS MY *ADOPTED* FATHER.
AND THAT I HAVE BIOLOGICAL PARENTS SOMEWHERE OUT THERE.
I TRAVEL HALFWAY AROUND THE WORLD *LOOKING* FOR MY BIOLOGICAL FATHER...
...AND I FIND--OF ALL THE PEOPLE ON THE PLANET--*YOU.*
TWENTY LONG YEARS LATER, I FIND *YOU* WHERE MY *FATHER* SHOULD BE.

TELL ME, CASSANDRA.
WHO IS HE?
WHO IS MY BIOLOGICAL FATHER?

COME ON, "HONEY POT"...
TELL ME.

#1 VARIANT BY GABRIELE DELL'OTTO

#1 VARIANT BY SKOTTIE YOUNG

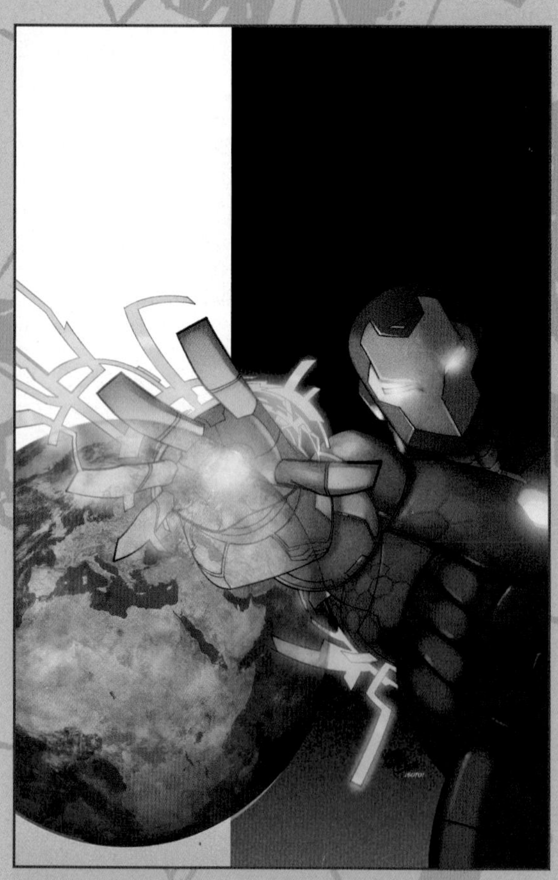

#2 CIVIL WAR VARIANT BY
PASQUAL FERRY & CHRIS SOTOMAYOR

#2 VARIANT BY KAMOME SHIRAHAMA

#4

ONE WEEK AGO.
--SO MANY QUESTIONS ARE STILL UNANSWERED ABOUT YESTERDAY'S AVERTED COSMIC-LEVEL THREAT.
EYEWITNESS REPORTS AND NUMEROUS AMATEUR VIDEOS SHOW CAPTAIN MARVEL AND IRON MAN WORKING IN TANDEM WITH WHAT SEEMS TO BE JUST ABOUT THE ENTIRE SUPER HERO COMMUNITY.
WE'VE REACHED OUT TO STARK REPRESENTATIVES FOR A COMMENT ON THE SITUATION, BUT AS OF THIS AIRING, WE HAVE NOT HEARD BACK.
OH, THAT REMINDS ME, MR. STARK--THERE HAVE BEEN NUMEROUS MEDIA REQUESTS ABOUT YESTERDAY'S AVERTED COSMIC-LEVEL THREAT--
REST ASSURED, AS SOON AS WE HAVE MORE INFORMATION WE WILL FORWARD IT ALONG TO YOU.
WOULD YOU LIKE TO GRANT AN INTERVIEW OR--?
STAR
IN OTHER NEWS, A TALKING DUCK CALLING HIMSELF HOWARD WAS ARRESTED AGAIN, THIS TIME FOR WEARING A RED SPANDEX--
FRIDAY?
YES?
I WANT TO START A SEARCH.
ON ANYTHING IN PARTICULAR?
MY PARENTS.
MY REAL BIOLOGICAL PARENTS.

I HAVE ALREADY STARTED THAT SEARCH.
YOU DID?
I DID!
WHEN?
AS SOON AS YOU DISCOVERED YOU WERE ADOPTED.

YOU STARTED LOOKING FOR MY BIOLOGICAL PARENTS BEFORE I ASKED YOU TO?
I KNEW YOU WERE GOING TO.
WHAT IF I DIDN'T?
MY TONY STARK PERSONALITY ALGORITHM SAID THERE WAS A VERY GOOD CHANCE YOU WOULD.
BUT WHAT IF I DIDN'T ASK YOU AND YOU WENT AND--?

YOU PROGRAMMED ME.
YOU PERSONALLY INSTALLED THE ALGORITHM BASED ON YOUR BRAIN PATTERNS AND BEHAVIOR MATRIX.
BUT WHAT--
IF YOU NEVER ASKED FOR THE SEARCH, YOU SIMPLY WOULD NEVER DISCOVER WHAT I FOUND.

DID YOU FIND MY REAL PARENTS?

BULGARIA.

UH, HEY, KIDS.
IS ANYONE-- UM, WHO'S IN CHARGE?

UH... ZDRAVEITE?

HI. I'M--
VIE STE TONY STARK.
YES, HI. AND YOU ARE--?
IRON MAN.
YOU ARE?
THAT'S AWKWARD, BECAUSE PEOPLE HAVE BEEN CALLING ME THAT FOR YEARS.

IZVINETE?
DO YOU SPEAK ENGLISH? I DO HAVE A TRANSLATOR PROGRAM FOR--
VHAT IS--VHY--VHAT IS IRON MAN DOING HERE?
YOU KNOW YOU ARE EEN BULGARIA.
YES, I FLEW HERE ON PURPOSE.

I'M--OH--I AM ANNA.
HI.
WHO CAN I SPEAK TO ABOUT--?
ME. I'M THE--I AM IN CHARGE. I AM THE ADMINISTRATOR.

I WAS--
IT SEEMS I WAS ADOPTED FROM HERE...MANY YEARS AGO.
WHEN I WAS A BABY.

NAISTINA LI?

I WAS TRYING TO RESEARCH THIS ON MY OWN BUT I RAN INTO AN UNUSUALLY HARD DEAD END.
I WAS WONDERING IF THERE WERE FILES? PAPER FILES? DECADES-OLD PAPER FILES?
I WAS WONDERING IF YOU--IF YOU COULD HELP ME.

I'M PRETTY GOOD WITH NUMBERS.
SOMEONE SOMEWHERE MUST HAVE TAKEN IT.
MY MOTHER WOULD HAVE NEVER--MY DAD...MY DAD WAS S.H.I.E.L.D. MY DAD TOOK IT.
HE'S THE ONLY ONE WHO KNEW ABOUT THE ADOPTION.
NO.

STILL NOTHING, MEESTER STARK?
IT'S-- IT'S JUST NOT HERE.
I TOLD YOU--NO ONE HAS BEEN DOWN HERE IN YEARS.
OLL OF OUR CASES SINCE I HAVE STARTED VORKING HERE HAVE BEEN ON COMPUTER. DIGITAL.
ARE YOU SURE YOU'RE LOOKING IN THE RIGHT YEAR?
YEAH...
NO?
I MEAN... YOU WERE ADOPTED FROM SOMEONE.
WHOEVER GAVE YOU UP.
THEY KNEW.
YOU KNOW, THAT'S THE KIND OF THING I USUALLY THINK OF.
IT'S INTERESTING HOW I'M HAVING TROUBLE DOING THAT ABOUT *THIS.*
INTERESTING.
"I LOVE YOU."

AUCKLAND, NEW ZEALAND
TWENTY YEARS AGO.
TONY!
LISTEN TO ME.
IT'S NOT EASY FOR ME TO SAY THOSE WORDS!
AND YOUR PARENTS? THEY KNOW WHERE YOU ARE, DON'T THEY?
THEY DO.
SO YOU DIDN'T EVEN RUN AWAY WITH ME.
I DON'T HAVE THE SAME HOSTILITY TOWARDS MY PARENTS AS YOU HAVE TOWARD YOUR FATHER.
YOU KNOW THAT.
YOU USED ME TO GET TO MY FATHER.
AND IT WAS SUCH A STUPID WASTE OF TIME.
I BARELY EVEN SPEAK TO HIM AND--AND WE NEVER EVEN TALKED ABOUT MY FATHER.
YES, WE DID.
I NEVER TALK ABOUT HIM.
IT'S ALL YOU EVER TALK ABOUT.

TONY, PLEASE...
YOU WERE USING ME, CASSANDRA.
I REALLY WOULDN'T CALL IT THAT.
OH, GOOD. SEMANTICS.
I FELL IN LOVE WITH YOU.

DAMN IT, CASSANDRA! HE WAS RIGHT? MY FATHER WAS RIGHT?!
ONLY IN THE BEGINNING. YOU'RE NOT LISTENING TO--
THAT HYDRA ATTACK.
WAS IT EVEN REAL?

REAL?
WAS IT?
I--I DON'T KNOW.
YOU DON'T KNOW?
DOESN'T THE FACT THAT YOU DON'T EVEN KNOW IF THE TERRORIST ATTACK ON YOUR FAMILY WAS REAL OR SOMETHING YOUR FAMILY DID TO SCREW WITH ME TELL YOU ANYTHING ABOUT THE QUALITY OF YOUR FAMILY?

GOOD! FINE!
GO BACK TO THEM.
BUT LISTEN TO ME VERY CAREFULLY... I DON'T KNOW YOU. I DON'T NEED YOU.

I LOVE YOU.
STOP SAYING THAT AS IF IT--

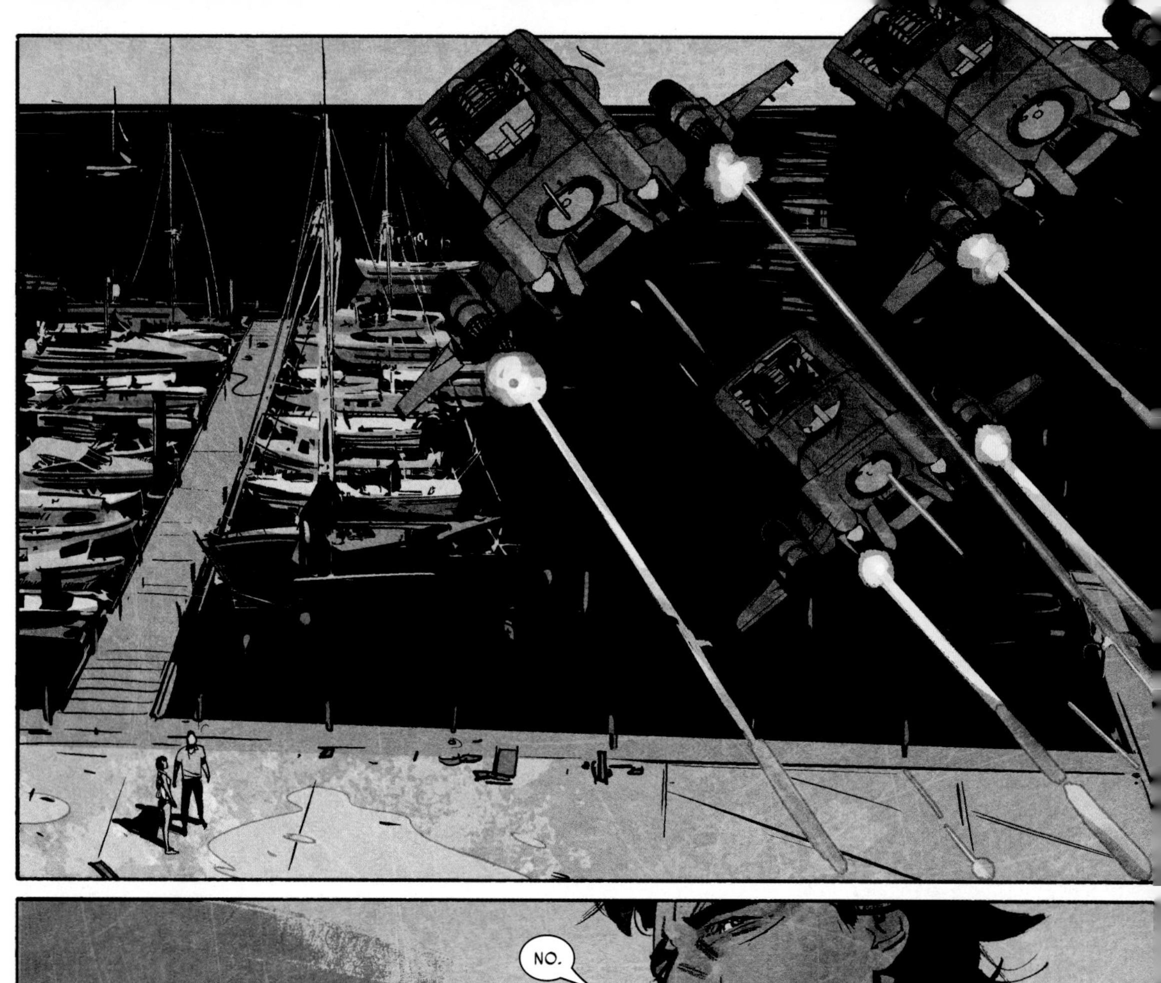

NO.

DAD.
GET AWAY FROM HER, TONY.
SHE'S A TERRORIST.

I HAVE THIS UNDER CONTROL, DAD.
GET IN THE CAR!
DAD!

YOU'RE EMBARRASSING ME AND YOU'RE EMBARRASSING YOURSELF!
AND YOU, TOOTSIE, YOU'RE NOW IN THE CUSTODY OF S.H.I.E.L.D.

MISTER STARK, I--
SHUT UP!
DUGAN?

HANDS ON YOUR HEAD, LITTLE LADY!

DAD?
TONY, ZIP IT!
YOU'VE COME THIS CLOSE TO CREATING AN INTERNATIONAL--
DAD?!
LET THE AGENTS OF S.H.I.EL.D. DO WHAT THEY NEED TO--

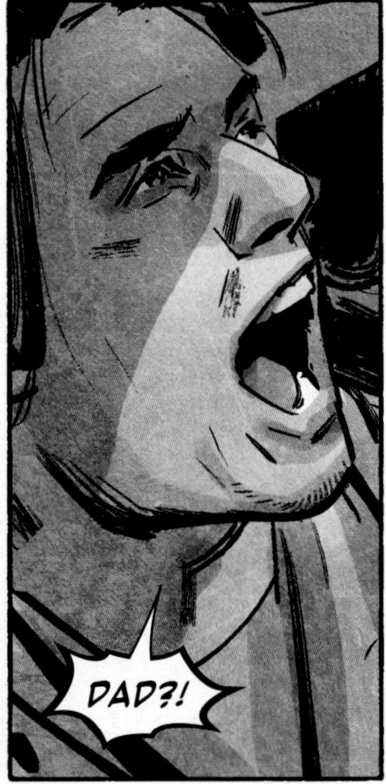
DAD?!

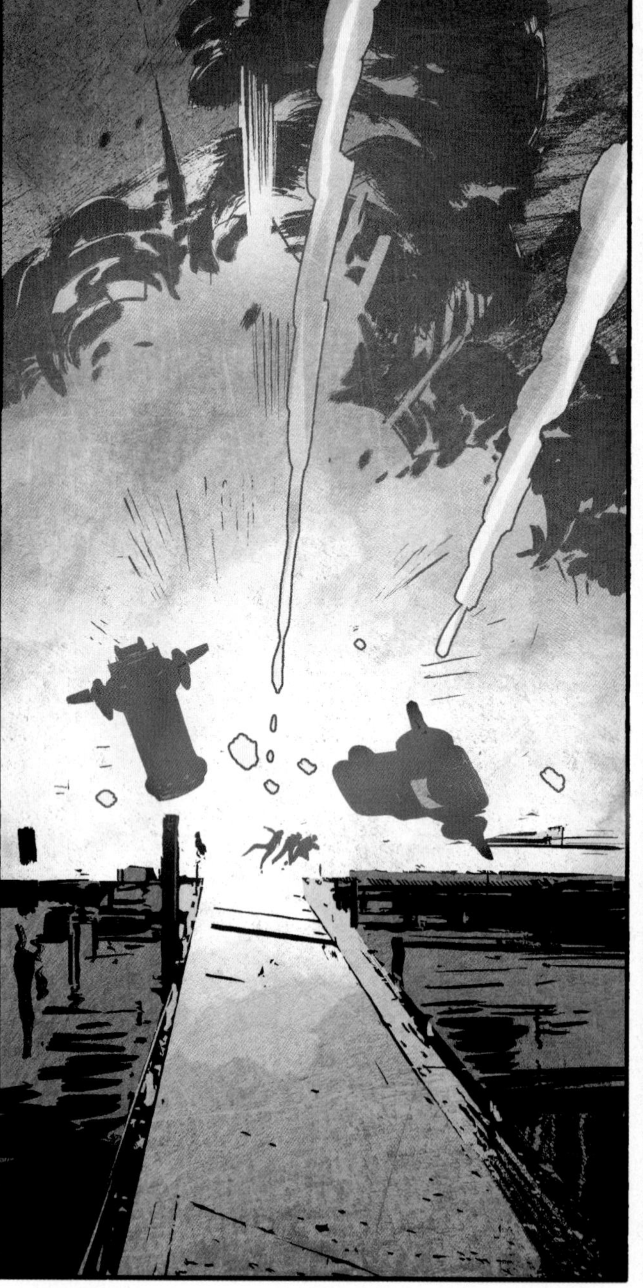

CASSANDRA!

THIS IS DUGAN!
WE NEED IMMEDIATE AND POWERFUL AIR SUPPORT!
WE ARE UNDER FIRE! IN THE OPEN!

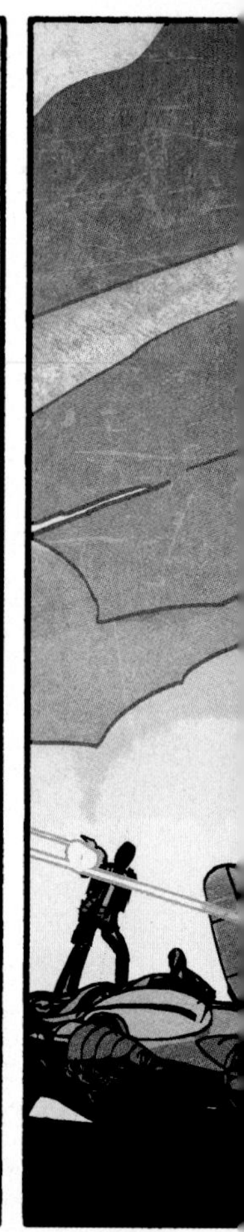

BUDDABUDDABUDDA
BUDDABUDDABUDDA

LET GO OF ME!
SHUT UP, TONY!

WE HAVE THE TARGET.
SUPREME HYDRA SAYS WE DON'T LEAVE WITHOUT TAKING OUT THE STARKS.

AAGGH!
STOP SCREAMING!
WE'RE SAFE IN HERE!
CASSANDRA!

CASSANDRA!

BUCHAREST.
GILLESPIE COMPOUND.
TODAY.
CASSANDRA...
WHERE (AND WHO) IS MY BIOLOGICAL FATHER?

DAMN YOU.
ROLES REVERSED? EVEN AFTER ALL THESE YEARS AND ALL THE WHATEVER...
...I WOULD TELL YOU.

WHILE YOU TRY TO FIGURE OUT YOUR NEXT MOVE...
...HOW ARE *YOUR* PARENTS?

DEAD.

OH.
WELL...
ANYWAY, BACK TO ME...

TWENTY YEARS.
YOU DON'T WANT TO ASK ME, NOW THAT WE'RE ALONE, HOW I AM STILL ALIVE?
WELL, EITHER HYDRA HELD YOU FOR RANSOM AND YOUR PARENTS PAID IT...
...OR YOUR PARENTS FAKED THE WHOLE THING SO THEY COULD GRAB YOU FROM S.H.I.E.L.D. WITHOUT LEAVING A TRAIL DIRECTLY BACK TO THEM...
...OR YOU STAYED WITH HYDRA AND NOW YOU DO THIS.
EITHER WAY, I DON'T THINK I ACTUALLY CARE.
YOU CARE.

I GUESS WHAT I MEAN IS, IT DOESN'T REALLY MATTER.
YOU'RE HERE, YOU'RE IN MY WAY AND I WANT ANSWERS.
AND THE FACT THAT YOU JUST *WILL NOT* ANSWER MY QUESTION MEANS YOU THINK I DON'T KNOW YOU HIT A LITTLE HIDDEN SECRET BUTTON AND ALERTED YOUR CREW OF MANDROIDS TO GET OVER HERE AND RESCUE YOU AND TAKE ME OUT.

YOU'RE GOOD.

IN THIS CONTEXT, NOT TO BRAG, I'M ACTUALLY THE BEST.
THE MANDROIDS' E.T.A. IS THREE MINUTES.
THREE MINUTES FOR YOU TO CHOOSE TO DO RIGHT BY ME.

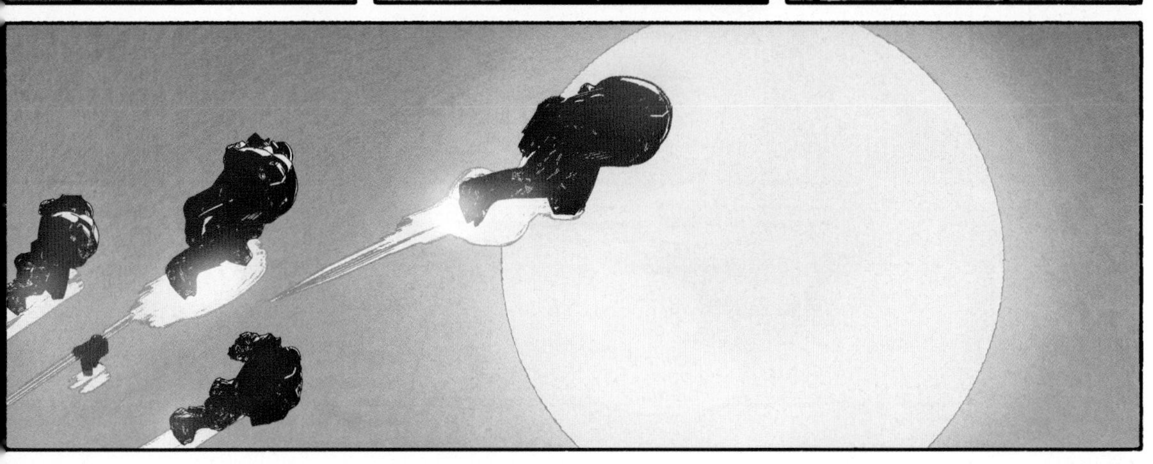

THREE MINUTES TO CONVINCE YOU...
...THAT I TRULY...
...HAVE NO IDEA WHAT YOU ARE TALKING ABOUT.
I DIDN'T EVEN KNOW YOU WERE ADOPTED.
IT'S A NEW TWIST.

WELL, TONY, I WISH I COULD HELP YOU.
AND I WISH YOU'D BELIEVE ME.

YOUR HEART RATE AND BODY TEMPERATURE SAY YOU ARE TELLING THE TRUTH.
OR YOU'RE A SOCIOPATH.
OR BOTH.

I HAVE WATCHED YOU ALL THESE YEARS.
WATCHED YOU TURN INTO AN AVENGER. A SUPER HERO.
WHEN YOU *CREATED* THE AVENGERS, I THOUGHT: THIS IS IT. ANY MINUTE NOW, WE WILL CROSS PATHS AGAIN.

AND WHEN YOU TOOK OVER S.H.I.E.L.D., I SAID TO MYSELF: THIS IS IT. THIS IS WHERE WE CROSS PATHS AGAIN.
BUT...
...IT NEVER HAPPENED.
YOU'RE THAT GOOD, I GUESS.
HOW DID YOU DO THAT BY THE WAY?

WHEN THE IMMEDIATE COMPETITION IS HELL-BENT ON DRESSING IN GREEN UNIFORMS AND YELLING OUT THEIR NAME...
...OR TRAIPSING AROUND IN BRIGHT YELLOW BEEKEEPER HATS AND MAKING BOLD MOVES...
YEAH...
IT'S PRETTY EASY TO SLICE OFF A CORNER OF THE WORLD WEAPONS MARKET WITH THE PROMISE OF DISCRETION.
AND FOR THE PEOPLE I DEAL WITH...

AND YET, MANDROIDS.

THAT YOU WOULDN'T HAVE EVEN KNOWN ABOUT IF YOU WEREN'T HERE LOOKING FOR YOUR DADDY.
A COINCIDENCE.
THEY *DO* HAPPEN.

EITHER WAY...
THIS.
IT FEELS LIKE IT ***MEANS*** SOMETHING.
MAYBE.
OKAY, I HAVE TO ASK...
...DO YOU EVER THINK ABOUT ME?

YOU'RE FAMOUS.
YOU'RE EVERYWHERE ALL THE TIME.
I COULDN'T *NOT* THINK ABOUT YOU.

I THINK ABOUT YOU ALL THE TIME.

I WONDER IF ANY OF IT IS TRUE.
WHAT?
THIS STUFF ABOUT BEING ADOPTED.

OF COURSE IT IS.

WE HAVEN'T SPOKEN IN MANY YEARS, BUT IF YOUR RELATIONSHIP WITH YOUR FATHER REMAINED AS TORTURED AS IT WAS WHEN WE WERE YOUNG...I WONDER IF YOU JUST REALLY WANT THIS ADOPTION TO BE TRUE.

CALL THEM OFF, CASSANDRA.

I CAN'T.
MY ENTIRE LIFE'S WORK IS WRAPPED AROUND STRENGTH.
IF I LET THIS GO...IF I LET YOU WALK AWAY...
...I'M RUINED.
YEAH.
SO, YOU GOT A HUSBAND? WIFE? KIDS?
TIME'S UP, TONY.
YEAH...

#5

THE FUNERAL FOR HOWARD STARK.
TWENTY YEARS AGO.

STARK MANSION.

KID.
HELL OF A FUNERAL, CAP'N FURY.
IT WAS.
HELL OF A FUNERAL.

YOU KNOW WHAT I LIKE? I LIKE THIS WHOLE "AFTER FUNERAL" THING.
THERE'S "THE FUNERAL" FOR ALL THE RIFFRAFF, LIKE THE PRESIDENT...
...AND THEN THERE'S THIS THING WHERE YOU CLANDESTINE OPERATIVES ALL COME OVER AND DRINK THE PLACE DRY.

OH.
YOU'RE DRUNK.
YES!
AND I PLAN TO STAY THAT WAY.
YOUR FATHER LOVED YOU VERY MUCH.

HA HA!
HA HA HA.
OH, MAN...

HERE'S A LIST OF THINGS HE LOVED:
HE LOVED THE SOUND OF HIS OWN VOICE.
END OF LIST.

YOU REALLY THINK HE DIDN'T LOVE YOU?
ONLY BASED ON ANY AND EVERYTHING HE EVER SAID OR DID.
REALLY?
BECAUSE JUST YESTERDAY I WAS CLOSING HIS BLACK FILES--GOING OVER ALL THIS INTEL ABOUT YOUR FATHER...
...AND ALL I SAW WAS A PARADE OF HERCULEAN ACTS OF FATHERLY KINDNESS AND SELFLESS SACRIFICE.

NOW WHO'S DRUNK?
HE WAS A TOUGH SON OF A BITCH.
I'LL GIVE YOU THAT.
TOUGH? HE WENT OUT OF HIS WAY TO DESTROY ANY CHANCE OF ME BEING HAPPY. EVER.
OUT OF HIS WAY!

LET GO OF ME!

COME ON!
SHE LOVED ME.
SHE LOVED ME.
AND HE--HE JUST COULD NOT LET IT BE.

OH, THE AUCKLAND INCIDENT. THE GILLESPIE GIRL.
I REMEMBER THAT ONE.
I HATE YOU SPIES.

YOU THINK HE MESSED THAT UP FOR YOU?
HE TRAVELED HALF-WAY AROUND THE WORLD SPECIFICALLY TO #$%#$% UP MY ONLY CHANCE AT REAL--
HE--HE JUST COULD NOT LEAVE IT ALONE.

YEP.
HE WAS A TOUGH ONE.
THING IS, I READ THAT REPORT BECAUSE S.H.I.E.L.D. AGENTS WERE INVOLVED...
...IN FACT, ONE DIED IN THAT LINE OF FIRE.

SURE, I CAN SEE HOW IT LOOKS LIKE HE TORTURED YOU FOR SPORT.
FATHERS AND SONS AND ALL THAT.
MINE WAS NO PICNIC.
BUT CONSIDER THIS...

...MAYBE HE TRAVELED HALFWAY AROUND THE WORLD TO THROW HIMSELF ON TOP OF YOU WHEN HE KNEW HYDRA WAS GOING TO TRY AND POP YA.
MAYBE HE TRAVELED HALFWAY AROUND THE WORLD WITH AN ELITE SQUAD OF AGENTS TO RESCUE YOU.
TO SAVE YOU.

LET GO OF ME!
SHUT UP, TONY!

NOW, WHAT WOULD YOU CALL THAT?

LISTEN...
I KNOW HE'D WANT ME TO SMACK THE CRAP OUT OF YOU FOR DIVING HEADFIRST INTO A BOTTLE.
BUT...IT'S A FUNERAL.
YOU'RE ALLOWED.
TODAY.

TOMORROW?
YOU GOT ALL THE SMARTS AND MONEY IN THE WORLD.
DO SOMETHING.
DO SOMETHING NO ONE ELSE CAN.

PFT.
SCREW YOU AND SCREW HIM.
"TIME'S UP, TONY."

BUCHAREST.
GILLESPIE COMPOUND.
TODAY.
MY MANDROIDS HAVE SURROUNDED THE COMPOUND.
YEAH...
THE SAME MANDROIDS THAT RIPPED THE ARMOR RIGHT OFF YOUR BODY.
BUT I WANT YOU TO KNOW, TONY, I WOULD HAVE NEVER COME AFTER YOU.
I WOULD HAVE NEVER BROUGHT THIS ON YOU.
YOU DID THIS.
YOU BROUGHT THIS ON YOURSELF.

OKAY.
OKAY?
OKAY! A DEAD MAN'S DYING WISH, CASSANDRA...
YOU EVER THINK ABOUT ME?
OF COURSE.
EVERY DAY?
EVERY--? NO.
I HAVE A *LIFE.*
OUCH.
BUT...

...MAYBE MORE OFTEN THAN I MIGHT WANT TO ADMIT.
HONESTLY? I THINK ABOUT YOU EVERY DAY.
EVERY DAY. AND I SINCERELY THINK MY LIFE IS CRAZIER THAN YOURS.

IT WAS NOT MEANT TO BE.
GOODBYE, TONY.

THOSE MANDROIDS ARE REALLY NICE TECH.
REALLY IMPRESSIVE DESIGNS.
AND I DON'T IMPRESS EASY.

BUT CLOSED CODE SYSTEMS?
I WOULD HAVE TRIED TO TALK YOU OUT OF THAT.
WHY?
THEY ARE UNTRACEABLE. UNHACKABLE.
WELL, I'VE ACTUALLY TRAVELED FROM ONE END OF THE GALAXY TO THE NEXT.
AND I HAVE LEARNED ONE UNDENIABLE TRUE-ITY...

...NOTHING IS UNHACKABLE.

BOOM
WHAT DID YOU DO?

WHAT THE HELL?
I'M NOT DOING THIS! I'M NOT IN CONTROL.
SHIELDS ARE DOWN!
BOOM
BOOM
BOOM
BOOM

WHAT DID YOU DO?
LISTEN, IT'S A *GOOD* SYSTEM.
IT TOOK MY A.I. ALL THIS TIME TO HACK INTO IT.
BUT IT'S HACKED.
IT'S DONE.
YOU'RE DONE.

FABOOM
FABOOM
BOOM

DAMN YOU!
BAM
BAM
BAM

CLOAKED ARMOR, I *TOLD* YOU...
...WASTE OF GOOD BULLETS.
PING
PING
SIT DOWN.
BE CIVILIZED.

FABOOM

BASTARD!
AND NOW SHE'S RUNNING.
BECAUSE SHE KNOWS I WON'T CHASE AFTER HER.

AND SHE'S RIGHT.

FRIDAY, WILL YOU DO ME A FAVOR? I CAN'T DO IT.
I THOUGHT YOU'D NEVER ASK, BOSS.

VRRROOOOMMMM
I WOULDN'T DO THAT.

AAHH!

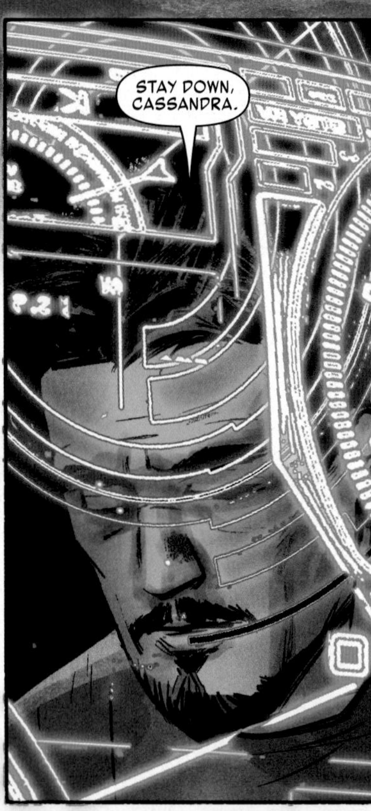
STAY DOWN, CASSANDRA.

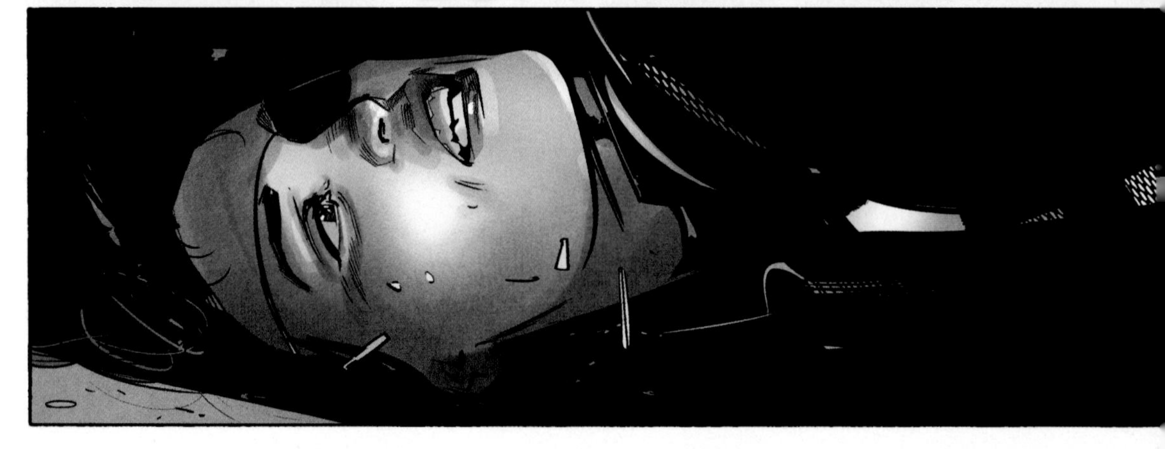

I FEEL I SHOULD INFORM YOU THAT YOU ARE NOW IN THE CUSTODY OF S.H.I.E.L.D.
WHICH WAS, IN PART, FOUNDED BY HOWARD STARK.
INTERESTING HOW THAT ALL KIND OF WENT FULL CIRCLE.

THIS IS NOT WHAT I CAME HERE FOR.
OH, SPEAKING OF WHICH, THERE ARE A COUPLE OF MESSAGES FROM ANNA.

ANNA?
FROM THE ORPHANAGE IN BULGARIA.

SOFIA, BULGARIA.
MEESTER STARK!
THERE IS TWO OF YOU NOW?
OH, DON'T MIND THAT.
YOU CALLED?
VELL, I WAS VERY FRUSTRATED, VERY FRUSTRATED, THAT YOUR RECORDS VERE SOMEHOW NOT EEN OUR FILES.
IMAGINE HOW I FELT.

VELL, AFTER YOU LEFT, I DEED SOME DIGGING.
ДЕЛО

WHAT IS THIS?

DIGGING AROUND IN THE BASEMENT, THERE WERE THREE MEESSING NUMBERED FILES FROM AROUND THE YEAR YOU THINK YOU WERE BORN.
I TOOK THE MEESSING NUMBERS AND CALLED THE LOCAL HOSPITAL ADMINISTRATORS.
ALL LOVELY PEOPLE I'VE DEALT WITH OVER THE YEARS.

I VANTED TO SEE IF THEY HAD ANY CORRESPONDING MEESSING FILES OR ANYTHING OUT OF THE ORDINARY, ANYTHING THAT STOOD OUT.
AND THERE WAS ONE?
THERE WAS ONE.

IT HAS HAPPENED TWICE.
WHAT HAPPENED TWICE?
BABY IS BORN. SOMEONE FROM SOME "AGENCY" COMES AND TAKES THE BIRTH FILES.
NO.
OH, YES.
ONLY TWICE, BUT--
ДЕЛО

--THEY TAKE THE BIRTH FILES, BUT WE STILL HAVE THE MOTHER'S MEDICAL.
WHEN IT HAPPENED, MY PREDECESSOR PUT IT IN HER SAFE.
WHICH IS NOW MY SAFE.
SHE CALLED IT HER BLACK FILE. I KEPT IT, ALMOST FOR FUN.
ДЕЛО

BLACK FILE.

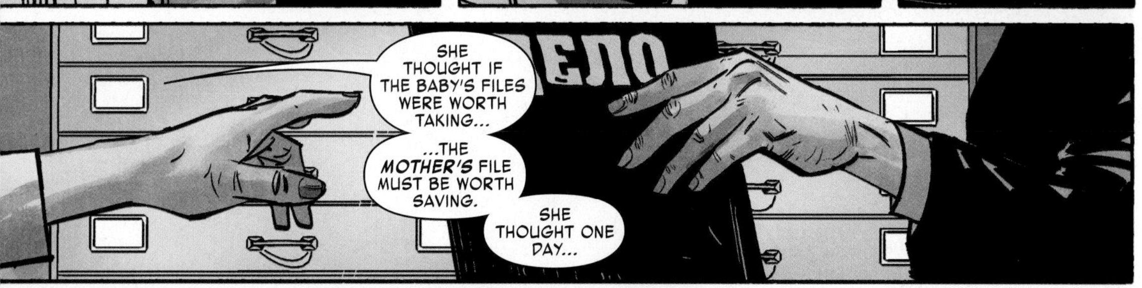
SHE THOUGHT IF THE BABY'S FILES WERE WORTH TAKING...
...THE MOTHER'S FILE MUST BE WORTH SAVING.
SHE THOUGHT ONE DAY...

ДЕЛО
...SOMEONE WOULD COME LOOKING FOR IT.
SHE SAID: IF IT WAS TODAY, COMPUTERS AND ALL, IT VOULD BE LOST TO THE MEN IN SUITS, BUT...

IS IT FOR SOMEONE SPECIAL?
WAS IT WORTH SAVING ALL THESE YEARS?

ДЕЛО

ДЕЛО

IT'S THE *LEAST* I CAN DO.
BUT--
YOU ARE THE IRON MAN.

HOW MANY TIMES HAVE YOU SAVED MY LIFE WITHOUT ME EVEN KNOWING IT?
IT'S *THE LEAST* I COULD DO.
THE VERY LEAST.

WELL, LADY, YOU JUST MADE A FRIEND FOR LIFE.
FRIDAY, THIS PLACE IS NOW UNDER OUR FINANCIAL CARE.
WHATEVER THEY NEED.
AND THEN SOME.

TONY, YOUR CASH FLOW IS NOT AT ITS BEST--
DON'T CARE.
SELL A PAINTING. SELL *ALL* THE PAINTINGS.
THIS WOMAN GETS WHATEVER SHE NEEDS FOR HOWEVER LONG SHE NEEDS IT.
FOOD, COMPUTERS, CLOTHES...CLEAN EVERYTHING.

HEY!
WHO HERE WANTS TO GO FOR A FLY?

SERIOUSLY, WHO WANTS TO BE IRON MAN?
FOR A MINUTE.
POZNAVATE LI SPIDER-MAN? TI MI E LUBIM.

WHAT DID HE SAY?
HE ASKED IF YOU KNEW SPIDER-MAN.
SPIDER-MAN IS HIS FAVORITE.

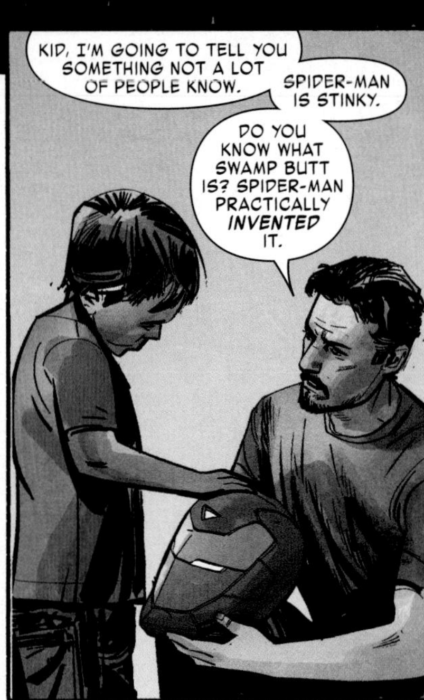
KID, I'M GOING TO TELL YOU SOMETHING NOT A LOT OF PEOPLE KNOW.
SPIDER-MAN IS STINKY.
DO YOU KNOW WHAT SWAMP BUTT IS? SPIDER-MAN PRACTICALLY *INVENTED* IT.

EES THAT SAFE?
THE ARMOR? SURE.
DON'T YOU VANT TO OPEN THE FILE?

I DO.
I WAS TRYING NOT TO LOOK DESPERATE.
I SEE THAT NOW.
EET'S A LITTLE WEIRD THAT YOU HAVEN'T OPENED EET YET.

PLEASEDON'TBETHEREDSKULL.
PLEASEDON'TBETHEREDSKULL.
PLEASEDON'TBETHEREDSKULL.
ДЕЛО

LONDON.

COME ON...
...YOU'VE SEEN THE HULK NAKED.
YOU CAN DO THIS.

UGH! THAT'S WHAT YOU THINK. THAT'S WHAT YOU THINK. THAT'S WHAT YOU THINK.
UGH!

UGH! THAT'S WHAT YOU THINK. THAT'S WHAT-- OH!
SORRY.
CAN I HELP YOU?

MAN, YOU LOOK REALLY FAMILIAR.
AMANDA?
AMANDA ARMSTRONG?
YES?
I'M TONY STARK.
OH, @#$@!
YOU ARE!
QUITE A FEW YEARS AGO YOU GAVE UP A BABY--
UM--
I SHOULD HAVE PHRASED THAT AS A QUESTION.
YEARS AGO...
...DID YOU GIVE UP A BABY FOR ADOPTION?
DID--DID YOU--
DID THE AVENGERS--
WHAT IS HAPPENING RIGHT NOW?

HI.

I'M SORRY TO JUST WALK IN HERE LIKE THIS...
...I THINK I MIGHT BE YOUR SON.

#6

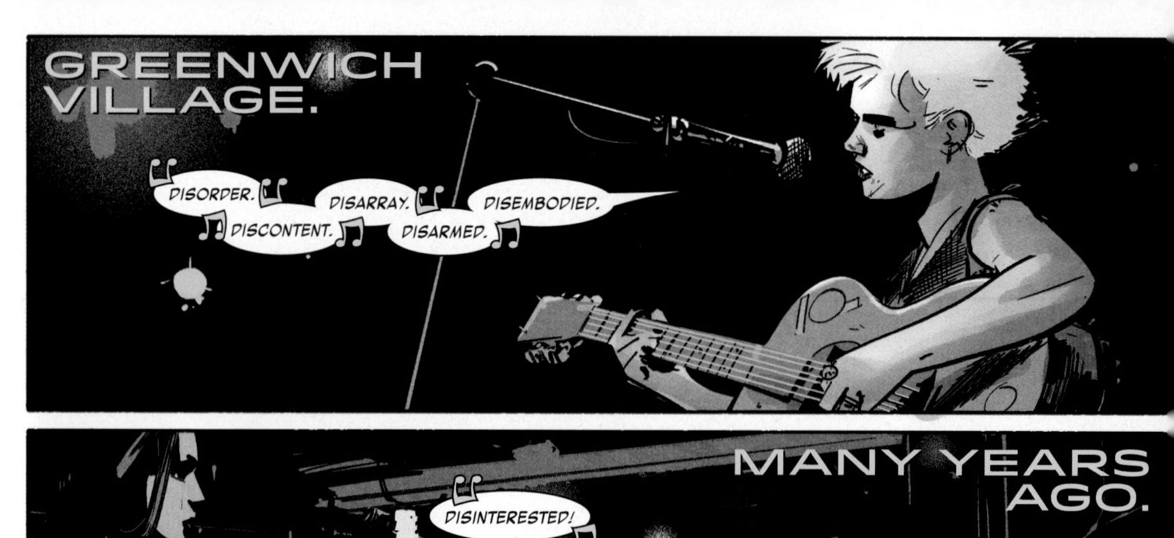
GREENWICH VILLAGE.
DISORDER.
DISCONTENT.
DISARRAY.
DISARMED.
DISEMBODIED.

MANY YEARS AGO.
DISINTERESTED!
DISINTERESTED!
DISINTERESTED!
WOO!

EXIT
DISINTERESTED!
DISINTERESTED!
DISINTERESTED!

UNLESS YOU'RE INTERESTED.
THEN MAYBE.

AMANDA STRONG?
YEAH.
NICE SET.
NOT REALLY.

I THOUGHT IT WAS REALLY--
I BROKE TWO STRINGS. THE MICROPHONE WAS POPPING MY P'S.
YOU COULDN'T TELL FROM THE BACK.

I'M SORRY. THANK YOU.
THANK YOU IS WHAT I SHOULD HAVE SAID.
STRONG. IS THAT YOUR REAL LAST NAME?
SHORT FOR ARMSTRONG.

I WOULD LOVE TO BUY YOU A DRINK.
UH... THANKS, BUT--
--BUT I THINK I'M, UH, GOING TO GO HOME AND LIGHT MY GUITAR ON FIRE.

OH! YOU SHOULD HAVE CLOSED THE SET WITH THAT.
ALMOST DID.
BUT THANKS.
I'M NOT REALLY--I MEAN, YOU'RE HOT AND ALL, BUT...
THANKS. I'M NOT HITTING ON YOU.

OH, UH.
SORRY AGAIN, THEN.
LET'S GO. DINNER'S ON ME.
WHAT IS THIS?

I WANTED TO TALK TO YOU ABOUT MAYBE GETTING YOU A RECORDING CONTRACT.
RECORDING CONTRACT?
ARE YOU WITH A LABEL?
NOT EXACTLY.
YOU A MANAGER?
NO.
I'M SORRY...
WHAT IS THIS?

SO...
...YOU WRITE YOUR OWN SONGS?
I'M SORRY...
WHAT IS YOUR NAME? WHAT DO YOU WANT FROM ME?
MY NAME IS VALENTINA.
VALENTINA ALLEGRA DE FONTAINE.
I'M AN AGENT OF S.H.I.E.L.D.
CAN--VALENTINA ALLEGRA DE FONTAINE?
CAN I SEE SOME CREDENTIALS?
NO.
NO?
AGENTS OF S.H.I.E.L.D. DON'T HAVE CREDENTIALS.
WE'RE SUPER-SPIES. SUPER-SPIES DON'T WALK AROUND WITH A LAMINATED CARD THAT SAYS *"SUPER-SPY."*
I'M SORRY.
WHAT--WHAT IS HAPPENING?
YOUR FATHER--HE WAS A FEDERAL AGENT.
MY DAD?
AND I KNOW THAT HE--
THIS IS ABOUT MY DAD?
IN A WAY.
IN **WHAT** WAY?

ISN'T EVERYTHING, ONE WAY OR ANOTHER, ABOUT OUR FATHERS?
I THINK I'M GOING TO LEAVE.
I'M SURE HIS DEATH IS STILL A SORE SUBJECT.
YEAH, YA THINK?
SIT.

MY DAD MEANT *EVERYTHING* TO ME-- *EVERYTHING--* AND YOU--
--YOU DON'T JUST--
I KNOW.
SIT.

WHAT? WHAT IS THIS? *WHAT?!*
I'M TRYING TO RECRUIT YOU.
FOR WHAT?
FOR... THE BETTERMENT OF MANKIND.

YOU-- YOU WANT *ME* TO BE AN AGENT OF S.H.I.E.L.D.?

YES.

YOU SAID YOU WANTED TO OFFER ME A RECORDING CONTRACT...AND NOW YOU WANT TO MAKE ME AN AGENT OF S.H.I.E.L.D....
...YOU DO SEE HOW THIS ALL SOUNDS CRAZYTOWN?

I AM OFFERING YOU A RECORDING CONTRACT.
A REAL ONE.
YOU GET TO MAKE A RECORD.
AND YOU GET TO TOUR.

TOUR?

AROUND THE WORLD.
AROUND THIS POLITICALLY FRACTURED, TERRORIST-LADEN, TOPSY-TURVY WORLD.

555-3253
TAKE THIS CARD. CALL THE NUMBER.
GEORGE MARTIN WILL ANSWER.
HE'LL PRODUCE YOU.

WHY ME?

I WAS TRYING TO TELL YOU.
YOUR FATHER. HE WAS A GOOD MAN. GUNNED DOWN IN THE LINE OF DUTY.
TAKEN OUT BY THOSE IDIOTS FROM A.I.M.
NO, IT WAS--
AND THIS MOTIVATION, ALONG WITH YOUR PSYCHOLOGICAL PROFILE, MATCHES SO MANY OF--
NO, IT WAS A--A DRUG CARTEL.

IT WASN'T.
A.I.M.
ADVANCED IDEA MECHANICS.
A BUNCH OF SCIENCE-BASED RELIGIOUS ZEALOTS.
A FANCY WAY TO SAY TECHNOLOGY-BASED TERRORISTS.
RIGHT NOW, MY BETTERS LIKE TO CALL THEM A DRUG CARTEL TO KEEP PUBLIC PANIC OVER A GROWING TECH-BASED TERRORIST CELL TO A MINIMUM.

DAMN.
INSANE.
EXCITING.

CALL THE NUMBER.
YOU'LL SEE THIS IS REAL.

HOW DO--?
HOW DO I KNOW?
I'M AN AGENT OF S.H.I.E.L.D.
ALL I KNOW ARE THINGS THE REST OF THE WORLD DOES NOT.

AND I KNOW YOU ARE A PERFECT CANDIDATE TO JOIN US.
INSIDE AND OUT. ON THE ROAD, HIDING IN PLAIN SIGHT.
YOU WANT ME TO AVENGE MY FATHER'S DEATH.
OH, NO.
NO.

WE TOOK CARE OF THAT.
THAT'S YESTERDAY'S PROBLEM.
THIS IS THE FUTURE WE'RE TALKING ABOUT.
YOU GET TO RECORD, TOUR, FOLLOW IN YOUR FATHER'S FOOTSTEPS...
...AND I GET A FREE COPY OF YOUR ALBUM.

FRESH JAMS presents
7:30 p.m. HALL OF ROCK
DY'S DEAD, DAVE
E ROUNDS RAPID
AMANDA STRONG
WAVE MOTION GUNS
T'RASHIN' 9
ts available at HALL OF ROCK
box office and by phone.
Tickets also available by post.
ed attached flyer to place order.
ONE YEAR LATER.
DISINTERESTED! DISINTERESTED! DISINTERESTED!
WOO!
WOO!
WOO!
YEAAAAAGGHHH!

NICE SET, 'MANDA.
REALLY TIGHT.
AW, THANKS, GUYS.
YOU GOT FLOWERS.

NO ONE EVER SENDS ME FLOWERS.
THEY GIVE YOU FREE DRUGS, IAN.
BUT FLOWERS WOULD BE NICE.
EVERY ONCE IN A WHILE.

WHO THEY FROM?
DOESN'T SAY.
WHAT A WANKER!
SIGN THE NOTE! YOU MIGHT GET SOME OUT OF IT.
THAT'S NOT HOW IT WORKS.
IT COULDN'T HURT.

HI.
YOU LOOK *EXACTLY* LIKE MY COUSIN GARY.

YOU KNOW... I GET THAT ALL THE TIME.

BUT NOW THAT I SEE YOU UP CLOSE, I REMEMBER...
...I DON'T HAVE A COUSIN GARY.

SIT.
DRINK?

FIRST THINGS FIRST.
I LOVE YOUR ALBUM.
I DON'T.
BUT THANK YOU.
I DO.
USUALLY, WHEN OUR BETTERS HAVE PLUCKED SOMEONE FROM THE WORLD OF MUSIC AND PUT THEM IN THIS WORLD, THEIR MUSIC (HOW DO I SAY THIS POLITELY?) MAKES MY EARS BLEED.
WAIT... THEY'VE DONE THIS BEFORE?
I'M NOT THE FIRST?
ONLY A COUPLE OF TIMES.
ANYONE I'VE HEARD OF?
THE GUY IN THE DUCK SUIT. WHAT'S HIS NAME?
NO.
YES.
NO! HE'S--HE'S SO GOOD.
HE'S AMAZING.
HE'S A PRAT.
YOU--YOU HAVE A VOICE. YOU HAVE SOMETHING TO SAY.
THANK YOU.
I'M JUDE.
HEY JUDE.
REALLY?

NOT REALLY. PUT IT IN YOUR POCKET.

IF I PUT IT IN MY POCKET TOO FAST, IT WILL LOOK LIKE I'M PUTTING IT IN MY POCKET TOO FAST.

IF I STARE AT IT, *ADMIRE* IT, IT LOOKS LIKE A THOUGHTFUL PRESENT TO A MUSICIAN WHO APPRECIATES SUCH THINGS AND NOT A S.H.I.E.L.D.-MADE ITEM DISGUISED TO LOOK LIKE SOMETHING SO INNOCUOUS.

I KNOW THE SCORE. THIS ISN'T MY FIRST TIME AT THE BALL.

HAMBURG.
INDRA
THE INDRA CLUB.
THE BEATLES PLAYED HERE, MAN.
THE *BEATLES.*

AND IT LOOKS LIKE THEY HAVEN'T WASHED THE PLACE SINCE.
IT'S A DUMP.
I'M PSYCHED.
IT'S MUSIC HISTORY. STOP.

JOHN LENNON CHANGED HIS UNDERWEAR HERE.
RIGHT HERE.

WOOF.
ROCK AND ROLL.

OH, MY GOD.
DO--DO YOU KNOW WHO I AM?
GIVE EET TO ME OR I KILL YOU RIGHT HERE.
I KNOW EXACTLY WHO YOU ARE, AGENT OF S.H.I.E.L.D.

YOU-- WHAT?
I-- I DON'T EVEN KNOW--

QUIET!
SMACK
AGGH!

GIVE EET TO ME!

GUNK!
CHUNK
BAM

SMACCKK
@#$@#!

HA!
BAM

OH, MY GOD!

BAM

AGH!

YOU $%&%!
I WAS GOING TO KILL YOU AFTER YOU HANDED EET OVER BUT NOW I'LL JUST KILL YOU.
NO!
I'LL FIND THE FILES.
NO!

BAM

AGH!

THIS IS THE STORY...

#@#$!

...OF
HOW TONY
STARK'S...

STILL GERMANY.

AH!

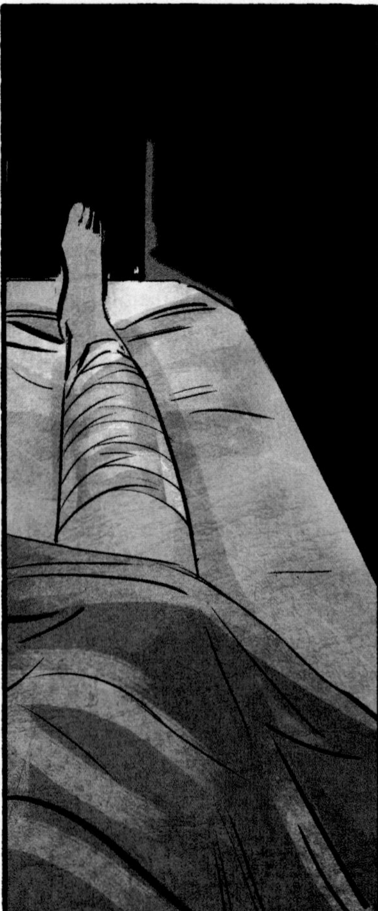

HEY!
JUDE!

...BIOLOGICAL PARENTS...

..MET.

DON'T.
SHOOT.

I'M ON YOUR SIDE, AMANDA.
BUT JUST A LITTLE TRADECRAFT...THAT BLANKET ISN'T BULLETPROOF.
WHERE ARE WE?
HOTEL. WE'RE LAYING LOW.
WHO WAS THAT THAT *SHOT* ME?
PROFESSIONAL ASSASSIN. OLLIE, I THINK WAS HIS NAME.
WE'LL GET THE REPORT FROM HQ.
I'VE NEVER BEEN SHOT BEFORE.
IT'S JUST A GRAZE.

A *BULLET* GRAZE.
WHAT WERE *YOU* DOING THERE?
HONESTLY? I CAME TO SEE YOUR SHOW.
YOU CAME ALL THE WAY TO GERMANY?
TO SEE *YOU* PLAY WHERE THE BEATLES PLAYED?
ABSOLUTELY.

HE WAS GOING TO KILL ME.
YES.
AND AFTER THE SHOW I-- I WAS HOPING TO CONVINCE YOU TO, YOU KNOW, MAYBE GO ON A DATE WITH ME.
THAT WAS, UNTIL I FOUND OUT YOUR COVER IS BLOWN.

HOW WAS MY COVER BLOWN?
WHAT HAPPENS NOW?

WE--
BOOOM
BOLLOCKS.

#7

STARK MANSION.
38 YEARS AGO.

MARIA, WE'LL TRY AGAIN...

BERLIN HOTEL.
37 YEARS AGO.
BOOM
BOLLOCKS.

BAM BAM BAM
AGH!

OH, MY GOD.
SHH.
JUDE!
NO NAMES.
SHH.

OH, MY GOD.
YOU-- YOU KILLED THE BELLMEN.

NOT BELLMEN.

HYDRA.
THEY KNOW WE'RE HERE.
HOW? WERE WE FOLLOWED?
OR JUST SET UP.
LET'S GO.
DO WE THINK THERE'S MORE?
WE HAVE TO CLEAR THE BUILDING, THEN I CAN CALL FOR AN EXTRACTION.
THIS IS INSANE.
THIS IS WHAT YOU SIGNED UP FOR.
CAN YOU MAKE IT TO THE ELEVATOR?
MY LEG IS THROBBING.
YOU CAN DO IT.
I HEAR SIRENS.
THEY'RE FOR US.

DIE SCHÜSSE KAMEN VON DORT.
RUFEN SIE DEN SICHERHEITSDIENST AN!
SPERREN SIE DAS GANZE GEBÄUDE UND ALLE AUSGÄNGE AB!

"SHOCKING NEWS OUT OF GERMANY..."

RECORDING ARTIST AMANDA STRONG, WHOSE FIRST SINGLE "DISORDER" IS CLIMBING THE CHARTS, WAS ATTACKED AT GUNPOINT BY AN OVERZEALOUS FAN BACKSTAGE AT A REHEARSAL FOR AN UPCOMING GIG IN HAMBURG, GERMANY.

DISORDER.
DISCONTENT.
DISARRAY.
DISARMED.
SECURITY FOR THE VENUE WAS ABLE TO SUBDUE THE ATTACKER AND AMANDA WAS ESCORTED OUT OF THE COUNTRY.
FILE FOOTAGE

STILL CLEARLY SHAKEN BY THE EVENT, THE SINGER-SONGWRITER SAT DOWN WITH US TO GIVE HER PERSPECTIVE ON THE GRUELING ORDEAL.

I THOUGHT I WAS GOING TO DIE.
THAT'S THE TRUTH.
HE HAD A GUN POINTED RIGHT AT MY FACE.
AND HE SHOT YOU IN THE LEG.
IT'S A GRAZE.

BUT STILL.
YES.
I WOULDN'T RECOMMEND IT.
OUCH!
SO I GUESS YOU'LL BE UPPING YOUR PERSONAL SECURITY.

YOU KNOW, I JUST HOPE THAT PEOPLE WHO NEED HELP, PEOPLE WITH ANGER ISSUES, REACH OUT TO GET THAT HELP.
WELL, LET'S TAKE A LOOK AT YOUR NEW VIDEO. THIS IS A WORLD EXCLUSIVE.
WELL DONE, AGENT.

YOU KEPT YOUR COVER. YOU KEPT YOUR COOL.
CAN'T ASK FOR ANYTHING MORE FROM AN UNDERCOVER AGENT...
AND YOU LIVED TO TELL THE TALE.
WHAT HAPPENS TO ME NOW?
AFTER A FEW MONTHS, WHEN THE OCCASION ARISES, WE CAN PUT YOU BACK TO WORK.

NO OFFENSE, AGENT DE FONTAINE, I'M NO EXPERT, BUT ISN'T MY COVER BLOWN?
WE ARE TAKING CARE OF THAT SITUATION AS WE SPEAK.

WHAT DOES THAT MEAN?
THERE WAS A LEAK. SOMEONE INSIDE S.H.I.E.L.D. SOLD YOU OUT TO HYDRA.
WE PLUGGED THE LEAK.
AND THE PEOPLE WHO WERE SOLD YOUR INFORMATION WERE TAKEN CARE OF, TOO.

DO I GET TO FIND OUT WHO SOLD ME OUT AND TRIED TO GET ME KILLED?
DOES IT REALLY MATTER WHO?
WELL... YES.
TO ME.

THE SITUATION IS UNDER CONTROL, YOU ARE SAFE, AND THIS MADE YOU A LITTLE MORE FAMOUS.
THAT'S ALL THAT MATTERS.

HOW DO YOU KNOW I'M SAFE?
BECAUSE THIS IS WHAT WE DO.
THEN HOW DID MY SECRET LEAK OUT?
BECAUSE THAT IS WHAT THEY DO.
I TOLD YOU, AMANDA...

THIS IS A *DANGEROUS* WORLD.
A WORLD *FULL* OF DOUBLE CROSSES, TRIPLE CROSSES...
EVERYONE IS *SURE* THEY ARE OWED MORE THAN THEY HAVE.
AND THEY WILL THROW ANYONE, EVEN SOMEONE AS TALENTED AS YOU, TO THE WOLVES IF THEY THINK IT WILL GET THEM WHAT THEY BELIEVE THEY DESERVE.

WELL, THANK GOD FOR JUDE.

HE *WAS* RIGHT THERE, WASN'T HE?

YES. HE WAS.
HE SAVED MY LIFE.
TWICE.

AND YOU, IT APPEARS, *FELL* FOR HIM.
STOP IT.

IT'S OKAY.
HE'S A HONEY.

68	78	94	3	CARS WITH THE BO DAVIS, J STONE, P KLEIN (R D
69	85	99	3	BOY, I'VE BEEN TOL C RODGERS, P SCHWARTZ (F
70	60	48	15	ALL FIRED UP K FORSEY, N GERALDO (K T
71	NEW ▶		1	DOMINO DANCING L.A. MARTINEE (N TENNANT
72	57	58	6	INSIDE A DREAM S HAGUE (J WIEDLIN, G CO
73		—	2	SPY IN THE HOUSE P.O. DUFFY (D WAS, D WAS)
74	77		3	DON'T BE AFRAID B BROMBERG, D WALKER (D
	90			BOUT A RE AUM (T CHAP
		—		S OF TRU LARMANN, F
			3	CAN'T WAIT G DUKE (SKYLARK)
	NEW		1	PLEASE DON'T BE AMANDA STRONG
		68	9	LONG AND LASTIN M MASSER (M MASSER, G
			2	I DID IT FOR LOVE B FORAKER (R BALLARD)
	NEW		1	NOT JUST ANOTHE D KORTCHMAR (I NEVILLE

NO.
IT WOULD APPEAR PEOPLE JUST LIKE YOUR SONG.

DISORDER.
DISCONTENT.
DISARRAY.
DISARMED.
DISEMBODIED.
DISINTERESTED!
DISINTERESTED!
DISINTERESTED!
WOO!

WE LOVE YOU, AMANDA!
WHHOOOO!
WHHOOOO!

THANK YOU.
THANK YOU ALL!
YOU KNOW, I USED TO SING THIS SONG IN A BASEMENT IN THE VILLAGE NOT FAR FROM HERE--
--TO A LOT LESS PEOPLE, AND--

WHHOOOO!

--I HAVE TO SAY...
...THIS IS MUCH BETTER.

NICE JOB, MISS ARMSTRONG.
THANK YOU, FRANK.
SEC
HEY!

HEY!
HEY! NO ONE COMES BACK HERE!
I'M A PAL.
WHOA! IT'S OKAY.

SERIOUSLY, IT'S OKAY.
QUITE A GRIP YOU HAVE THERE, YOUNG FELLA.
ARE YOU--?
JUST WATCH THE DOOR. I'M OKAY.

WELL, LOOK AT YOU.
I WAS WONDERING IF I'D EVER SEE YOU AGAIN.
ME?
LOOK AT *YOU.*

I WAS ON ASSIGNMENT.
CLEANING UP THE MESS IN GERMANY.
WHICH LED TO ANOTHER MESS AND ANOTHER...
IS IT CLEAN?
IT IS *SPARKLING* CLEAN.
AND NOW I HAVE SOME TIME OFF.

SO YOU THOUGHT YOU'D COME AND SEE THE SHOW?
I WAS WONDERING WHAT YOU WERE DOING.
WHEN?
NOW.
ACTUALLY, THAT WAS MY LAST SCHEDULED GIG FOR THE MONTH.

FANCY THAT.
HE SAYS, KNOWING FULL WELL THAT IT WAS.
I *AM* IN INTELLIGENCE.
WHAT DID YOU HAVE IN MIND?
DO YOU LIKE BOATS?
BOATS?

TWO YEARS LATER.

HEY JUDE.

REALLY? STILL?

AND THAT MUSTACHE IS A DEAL BREAKER.
YES, MA'AM. IT'LL BE GONE BY MORNING.
I'M SORRY I WAS GONE LONGER THAN I SAID.
THE GUY WITH THE EYEPATCH HAD OTHER PLANS FOR ME.
I AM GETTING SICK OF THAT MAN AND HIS EYEPATCH.

I HAVE A PRESENT FOR YOU.
THAT WASN'T IT?

I ALREADY HAVE A WATCH.
IT SHOOTS POISON DARTS.
THIS IS BETTER.

BETTER THAN A WATCH THAT SHOOTS POISON DARTS?

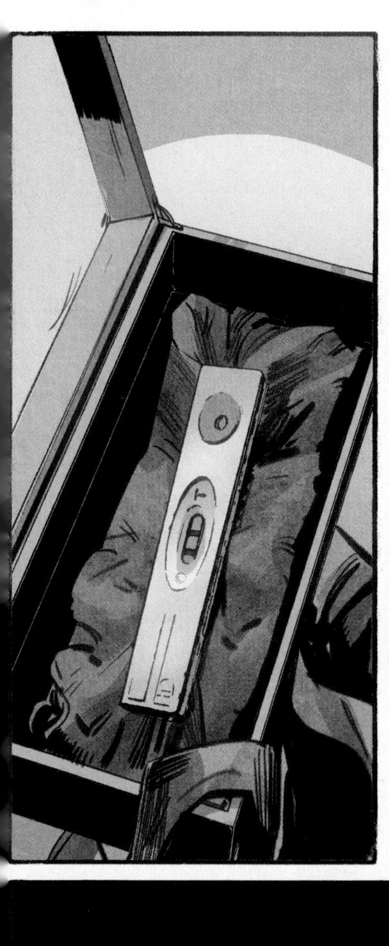
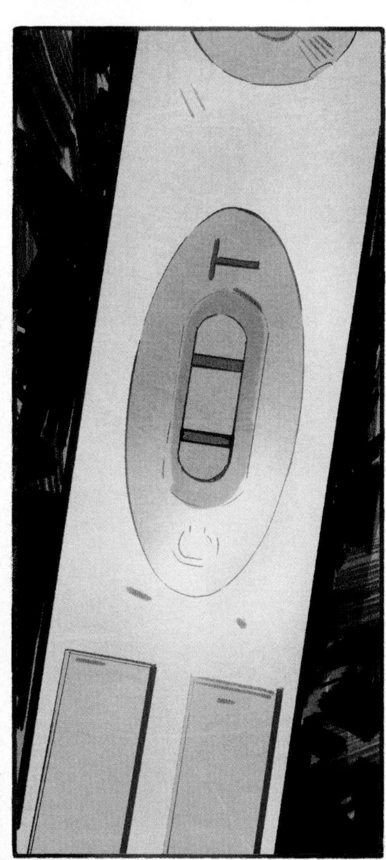

I PEED ON IT AND EVERYTHING.

WOW.

NINE MONTHS LATER...

OH, BABY, STOP WITH THE KICKING!

OH, MY GOD-- AM I?

OH, MY GOD.

I'M OKAY.

I DIDN'T WANT TO WAKE YOU.
OH, MY GOD.
I GOT IT.
I'M ALMOST DONE.
WHAT HAPPENED?

THIS STUPID JOB IS WHAT HAPPENED.
OH, BABY.
HOW ARE *YOU?*
ME? PREGNANT!
I'M SORRY I'M NOT AROUND.
ME, TOO.

WE SHOULD TALK ABOUT ALL OF THIS, *HUH?*
ABOUT OUR FUTURE PLANS.
BABY COMING.
I'M OUT.
I TOLD THEM I'M DONE.
THEY SAID: TOO BAD. PREGNANT WOMEN MAKE THE BEST AGENTS.

REALLY?
EXACT QUOTE.
I DO GET IT. BUT IT'S NOT WHAT YOU WANT TO HEAR...
WE CAN DISAPPEAR, YOU KNOW.
WE CAN?

RIGHT NOW.
TODAY.

WHAT WOULD WE DO FOR MONEY, HONEY?

I HAVE MONEY.

REALLY?
I HAD A HIT SINGLE AND I DON'T.
I'M TELLING YOU, I HAVE MONEY. WE CAN GET OUT OF HERE.
HOW DO YOU HAVE MONEY?

THAT THING THEY SAID TO YOU, ABOUT HOW YOU'D BE A GREAT AGENT PREGNANT?
THAT'S THE MOST HONEST THING THEY'VE EVER SAID. THAT'S HOW THEY THINK OF US.
THEY JUST USE US.

AND IF YOU THINK ABOUT IT...
...WHAT'S THE DIFFERENCE BETWEEN S.H.I.E.L.D. AND HYDRA, ANYWAY?
THEY'RE BOTH THE SAME.
NO.
ONE IS A BUNCH OF WHACKED-OUT TERRORISTS.

AND THE OTHER IS HYDRA.

STOP IT.

I'M SERIOUS.

WHAT ARE YOU SAYING?
HYDRA HAS MADE IT SO WE NEVER HAVE TO WORK A DAY IN OUR LIVES.
WE CAN GO *ANYWHERE* IN THE WORLD THAT YOU WANT.
WE CAN RAISE THE BABY *ANY WAY* THAT *YOU* WANT.
YOU AND ME.

WAIT, HOW DID--HOW DID *HYDRA* MAKE IT SO YOU CAN DO ANYTHING?
YOU'RE AN *AGENT OF S.H.I.E.L.D.*

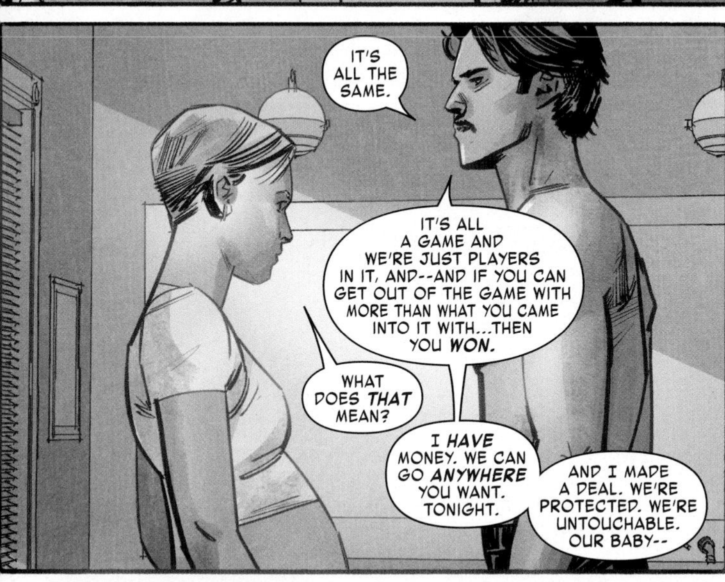
IT'S ALL THE SAME.
IT'S ALL A GAME AND WE'RE JUST PLAYERS IN IT, AND--AND IF YOU CAN GET OUT OF THE GAME WITH MORE THAN WHAT YOU CAME INTO IT WITH...THEN YOU *WON.*
WHAT DOES *THAT* MEAN?
I *HAVE* MONEY. WE CAN GO *ANYWHERE* YOU WANT. TONIGHT.
AND I MADE A DEAL. WE'RE PROTECTED. WE'RE UNTOUCHABLE. OUR BABY--

HYDRA SET YOU UP?
ARE YOU *WORKING* FOR THEM?

IT'S ALL THE SAME.

HYDRA MURDERS PEOPLE.
SO DOES S.H.I.E.L.D.
YEAH. *BAD* PEOPLE.
BELIEVE WHAT YOU WANT.
BUT YOU'RE BEING *INSANELY* NAIVE.

ARE--ARE YOU AN AGENT OF *HYDRA?*

YOU'RE JUST DESPERATE TO PUT LABELS ON EVERYTHING.

ARE YOU WORKING WITH HYDRA WHILE WORKING AS AN AGENT OF S.H.I.E.L.D.?

AND NOW WE CAN RAISE OUR BABY ANY WAY WE--

WHAT DO YOU DO FOR THEM?

HOW LONG HAS THIS BEEN GOING ON?
DOES IT MATTER?
I'LL TELL YOU WHEN YOU'RE BEING LESS JUDGMENTAL.

HOW *LONG?*
I THOUGHT YOU'D UNDERSTAND.

WERE YOU WORKING FOR THEM WHEN THEY SENT THAT ASSASSIN AFTER ME?

OF COURSE NOT.

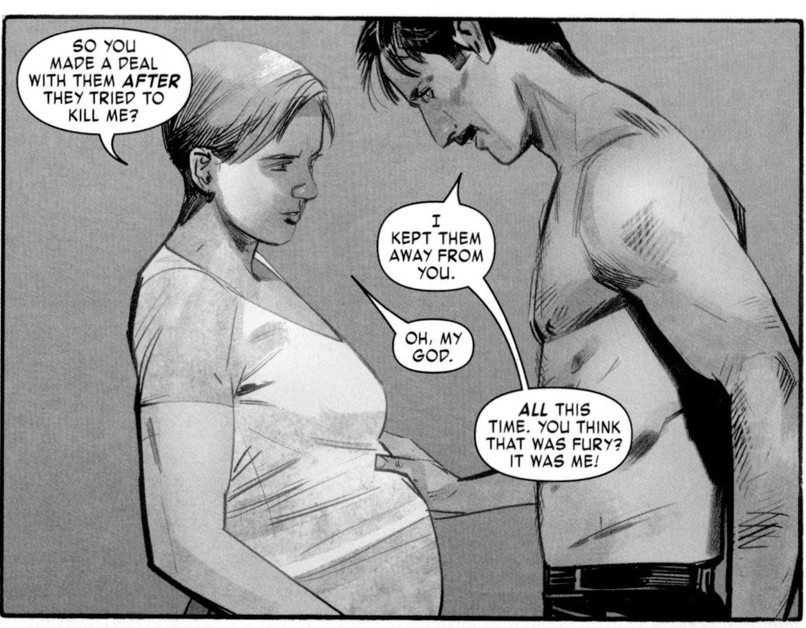
SO YOU MADE A DEAL WITH THEM AFTER THEY TRIED TO KILL ME?
I KEPT THEM AWAY FROM YOU.
OH, MY GOD.
ALL THIS TIME. YOU THINK THAT WAS FURY? IT WAS ME!

YOU KNOW ME.
YOU KNOW I WOULD NEVER PUT YOU OR THE BABY IN A SITUATION THAT WOULD--
THE BABY IS DUE NEXT WEEK.
AND THAT BABY WILL ALWAYS CONNECT US. ALL YOU NEED TO DO IS--

WHAT DO YOU DO FOR HYDRA, EXACTLY?
WELL, CLEARLY YOU'RE NOT IN THE MOOD TO HEAR ME.
YOU SELL THEM INTELLIGENCE?

YES.

YOU'VE SOLD AGENTS.
YOU'VE SOLD OUT OTHER AGENTS.
I'LL BE HAPPY TO DISCUSS THIS WITH YOU WHEN YOU'RE THINKING CLEARLY.
GRAB THE SCISSORS AND CUT THE GAUZE.

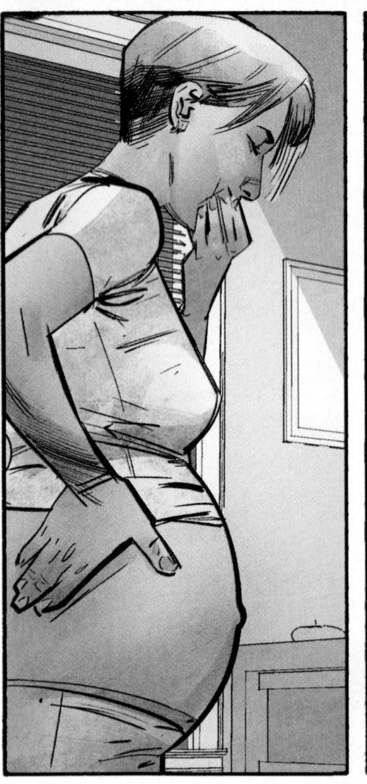

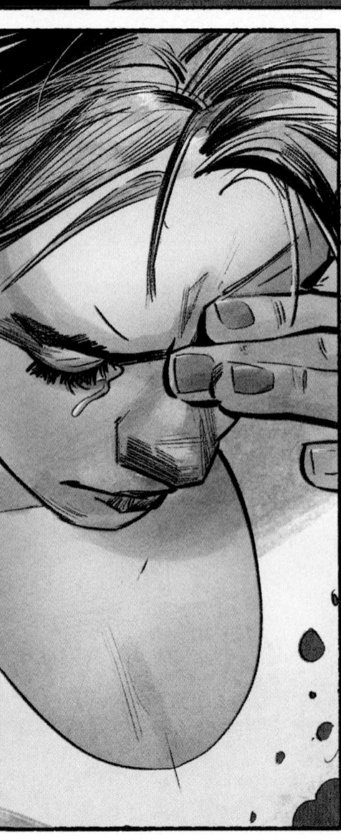

JACKPOT RECORDS.
YEAH, UH, I NEED SOMETHING CLASSICAL.

ARE YOU OKAY?

I WANT ONE FAVOR FROM YOU AND THEN YOU'LL NEVER SEE ME AGAIN.
I WANT YOU TO FIND...
...THIS BABY...
...A SAFE AND HAPPY HOME.

THAT'S--THAT'S NOT REALLY WHAT WE DO.

"DAMN RIGHT, WE *DON'T* DO THAT."

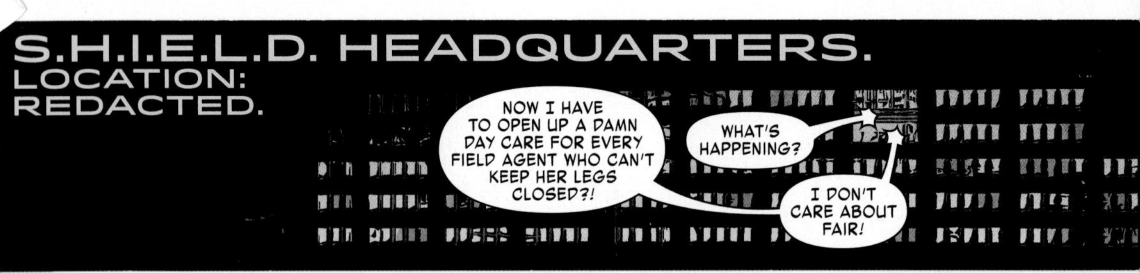
S.H.I.E.L.D. HEADQUARTERS.
LOCATION: REDACTED.
NOW I HAVE TO OPEN UP A DAMN DAY CARE FOR EVERY FIELD AGENT WHO CAN'T KEEP HER LEGS CLOSED?!
WHAT'S HAPPENING?
I DON'T CARE ABOUT FAIR!

NOTHING YOU HAVE TO WORRY ABOUT, MISTER STARK.
AN AGENT IN THE FIELD IS ABOUT TO DELIVER A BABY SHE DOESN'T WANT AND SHE WANTS US TO GET RID OF IT FOR HER.
A BABY? DOES THIS HAPPEN A LOT?
ALMOST NEVER.

WHAT DO YOU DO WHEN IT DOES?
WELL, WE DROP THE KID INTO AN ORPHANAGE SOMEWHERE IN EUROPE.
AND THEN?
AND THEN WE BURN THE FILES.

WHERE IN EUROPE?
"MARIA?"

MARIA!
WHERE IS SHE?
IN THE GARDEN, SEÑOR STARK.

HONEY, YOU KNOW HOW SOMETIMES I DO HUGE THINGS WITHOUT CONSULTING YOU?
I THINK I DID IT AGAIN.

MARIA...
LOOK AT ME...

HOWARD?
I THINK THIS COVERS BIRTHDAYS AND CHRISTMAS FOR AT LEAST TWO YEARS.
WHAT-- WHAT DID YOU DO?

YOU KNOW HOW YOU ALWAYS SAY IF SOMETHING IS MEANT TO BE, IT'S MEANT TO BE...
...AND I MAKE FUN OF YOU FOR IT?

IT--IT WAS MEANT TO BE.
OH, MY GOD! DOES-- DOES HE HAVE A NAME?
ANTHONY.
THE BIRTH MOTHER WANTS THE NAME TO REMAIN.
ANTHONY.

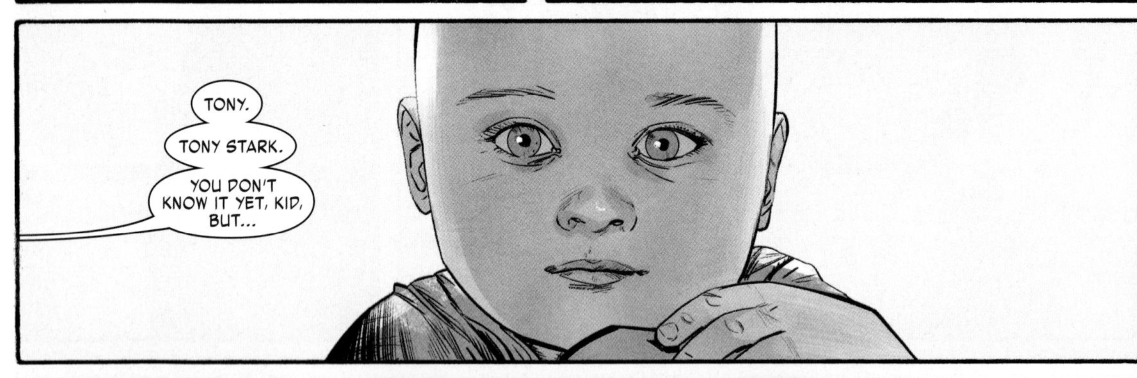
TONY.
TONY STARK.
YOU DON'T KNOW IT YET, KID, BUT...

"...YOU JUST HIT THE JACKPOT."
I'M SORRY TO JUST WALK IN HERE LIKE THIS...
I THINK I MIGHT BE YOUR SON.

WH-- WHAT?
HI.
OH, DEAR LORD.

BUT--BUT YOU'RE--YOU'RE *IRON MAN.*

AND I REALLY LOVE YOUR MUSIC.

OH MY GOD.

IT'S *VERY* NICE TO MEET YOU.

OH MY GOD.

IF YOU DON'T MIND...
...I WOULD LIKE TO GET TO KNOW YOU.

MY BOY.
TO BE CONTINUED...
IN INVINCIBLE IRON MAN!

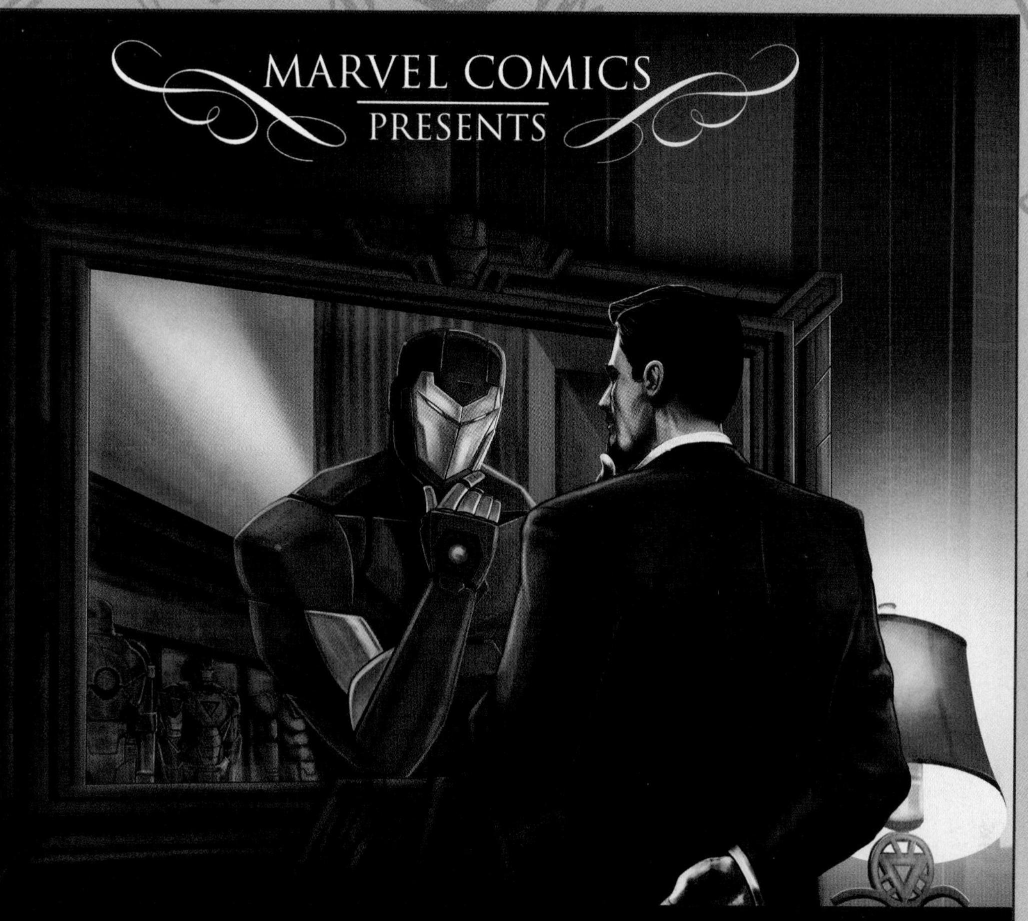

#1 HIP-HOP VARIANT BY MARCO D'ALFONSO

#3 VARIANT BY SKAN